ffing Birds, Pressing Plants, Shaping Knowledge

Natural History in North America, 1730–1860

MAGNOLIA *Acuminata.*

Stuffing Birds, Pressing Plants, Shaping Knowledge

Natural History in
North America, 1730–1860

Sue Ann Prince, Editor

American Philosophical Society
Philadelphia | 2003

Transactions of the American Philosophical Society
Held at Philadelphia
For Promoting Useful Knowledge
Volume 93, Part 4

Published for the exhibition
Stuffing Birds, Pressing Plants, Shaping Knowledge: Natural History in North America 1730–1860
Presented at the American Philosophical Society
Philosophical Hall, Philadelphia, Pennsylvania
20 June 2003–31 December 2004

Bibliographic information for items illustrated in this book may be found in the Checklist of the Exhibition on pp. 97–109.

ISBN: 0-87169-934-6
US ISSN: 0065-9746

Library of Congress Cataloging-in-Publication Data

Stuffing birds, pressing plants, shaping knowledge : natural history in North America
    1730–1860 / Sue Ann Prince, editor.
        p. cm.—(Transactions of the American Philosophical Society ; v. 93, pt. 4)
    Includes bibliographical references and index.
        ISBN 0-87169-934-6 (pbk.)
        1. Natural history—North America—History—18th century—Exhibitions. 2. Natural
    history—North America—History—19th century—Exhibitions. I. Prince, Sue Ann. II. Series

QH21.N7S78 2003
508'.097'09033—dc21   2003056004

Designed by ANN ANTOSHAK

FRONTISPIECE Pierre Jean François Turpin, *Cucumber Magnolia (Magnolia acuminata)*, after 1797. Watercolor, graphite, and ink. American Philosophical Society.

Table of Contents

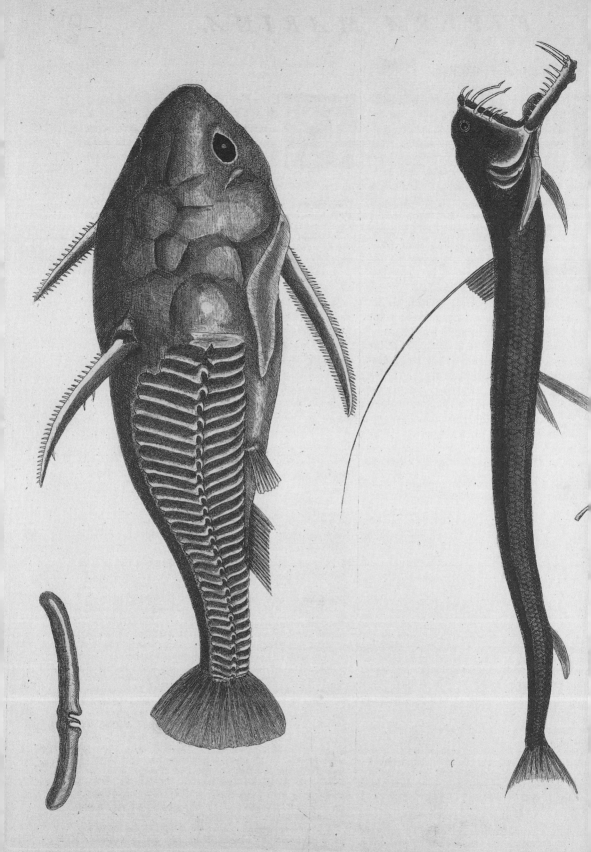

Foreword

This volume is published on the occasion of the exhibition *Stuffing Birds, Pressing Plants, Shaping Knowledge: Natural History in North America, 1730–1860.* It is the second public exhibition to be presented by the American Philosophical Society since the inception of a new public outreach program in 2001. Thanks to the launching of the program, Philosophical Hall, which was completed in 1789, is open regularly to the public for the first time since naturalist-artist Charles Willson Peale closed his museum there in the early nineteenth century.

The purpose of the exhibition program is to provide a public forum where the intersections of history, art, and science can be explored through objects in the Society's collections, together with materials on loan from other institutions. Exhibitions are documented through catalogues such as this volume, which is also part of the Society's quarterly *Transactions*, a series published without interruption since 1771.

The American Philosophical Society was founded by Benjamin Franklin in 1743 for "promoting useful knowledge among the British Plantations in America." The

OPPOSITE Mark Catesby, *The National History of Carolina, Florida, and the Bahama Islands . . .* , vol. 2 (2nd ed.), London: C. Marsh . . . , 1754. Supplement, Plate 20: *Vipermouth (Vipera marina) and Cataphractus americanus.* Pennsylvania Horticultural Society, on deposit at the American Philosophical Society.

first learned society on the North American continent, it was soon to emerge as an important player in the formation of the new national government, serving the role of an academy of science, a patent office, and a national library and museum. The inspiration for the current exhibition comes from the Society's early history. Many of the members, among them the founders and early presidents of the new country, participated in the practice of natural history as it was then understood. Thomas Jefferson, for example, who was president of the United States and the Society simultaneously, was a naturalist as well as a statesman.

Natural history in the eighteenth and early nineteenth centuries was a broad and fascinating endeavor, blending art and science in a national and even international effort to understand the natural world and every creature in it. This exhibition is unusual in bringing together many different kinds of materials: historical specimens collected and prepared by now well-known naturalists, manuscript materials, first-edition books, and artwork in the form of watercolors, drawings, and engravings. As such, the exhibition reveals the breadth of activities that the study of natural history once required, from the task of shooting or trapping animals for specimens to the linguistic task of naming and describing them and the artistic work of documenting them in drawings and watercolors.

Now that the American Philosophical Society has opened its doors to the public on an ongoing basis, it is committed to sharing its historic collections with a broad audience. We are extremely grateful to those who are helping us accomplish this goal, and we especially thank the Crystal Trust, the National Institutes of Health, the Richard Lounsbery Foundation, and the Dolfinger–McMahon Foundation (information as of 15 July 2003) for their generous support of *Stuffing Birds, Pressing Plants, Shaping Knowledge.*

FRANK H. T. RHODES, *President*
American Philosophical Society
Philadelphia, Pennsylvania

Acknowledgments

Many people have made possible the exhibition titled *Stuffing Birds, Pressing Plants, Shaping Knowledge: Natural History in North America, 1730–1860*. Thanks to the support and enthusiasm of lenders, scholars, and staff members at the American Philosophical Society, both the show and catalogue became larger and even more exciting than anticipated.

My debt to the members and staff of the American Philosophical Society is immeasurable. I am especially grateful to President Frank Rhodes and Executive Officers Mary and Richard Dunn, who have enthusiastically and unequivocally backed this project from the beginning. Without their support, it could not have been realized. I also am indebted to former Executive Officer Alexander Bearn, who had the vision to initiate an ongoing exhibition program at the Society. Member and Curator Henry A. Millon, advisor and mentor, provided unfailing encouragement, knowledge, and humor at just the right moments. Members of the exhibitions advisory committee that he chairs were generous in their counsel on behalf of the exhibition program: David Brigham, Elizabeth Cropper, Sheldon Hackney, Charles Ryskamp, and the late Kirk Varnedoe.

I also owe my gratitude to the Society's late Librarian Ted Carter and to Librarian Martin Levitt, both of whom provided essential support for the curatorial staff throughout the exhibition process. I am also indebted to the following staff members: Rob Cox, whose knowledge of the Library's collections is always an inspiration; Valerie-Anne Lutz, whose good cheer through endless details was invaluable; Roy Goodman, whose patience and help in finding materials was unfailing; conservators Hedi Kyle, Anne Downey, Denise Carbone, and Sharon Hildebrand, who deftly cleaned and prepared numerous objects for display; Mary McDonald, who provided editorial guidance on this catalogue; Frank Margeson, whose thoughtful photography contributed to every part of the project; Annie Westcott, who planned the opening festivities for the exhibition; Nanette Holben, who secured the necessary funds to make the project happen; and consultant Elaine Wilner, who succeeded in publicizing our work to a broad audience. I am also greatly indebted to framer and preparator Bill Severson, who helped ready numerous objects for display, and to education consultant Mary Teeling, who along with William Adair of The Rosenbach Museum & Library conceptualized an initial plan for launching an education program at the Society; Mary also created and developed a family gallery guide for this show. Her intuitive and intellectual savvy has been a guiding force throughout the development of interpretive materials.

My appreciation extends to many others at the Society, especially Frank Sabatini, whose good will and determination to get things right saw us through the final stages of preparation, and Carl Miller, who facilitated endless discussions, processes and negotiations. For all other staff members in both Philosophical Hall and Library Hall whose work supported our efforts but whom I am not singling out here, I offer my sincere gratitude. Finally, to all those working in the Curatorial and Exhibitions Department who endured tense deadlines with good cheer and provided consistently excellent work over many months, I offer my heartfelt thanks: Kevin Hatch and Shanin Dougherty, former and current assistant respectively; Jane Boyd, research associate and creator of the exhibition checklist; Katie Wood, exhibitions assistant; and Brian Gregory, museum education specialist. These talented people, along with interns Eric Gollannek, Emily Hage and Erin McLeary, constituted an unbeatable team. I salute them.

Beyond the Society, I would like to thank Amy Meyers, whose enthusiasm and generosity sustained me throughout the project. Our exhibition is an outgrowth of an earlier project of hers, and her natural history symposium (to be held at the Philadelphia Museum of Art in November 2004) will serve as its culmination. I also want to acknowledge catalogue authors Joyce E. Chaplin, Michael Gaudio, and Robert McCracken Peck for the thought-provoking essays they have provided.

Colleagues intimately involved in the design and production of both the exhibition and the catalogue also are to be congratulated. I am grateful to exhibition designer Stephen Saitas, whose exquisite taste, visual thinking, and sense of space transformed

groups of related objects into striking and intelligent displays. His patience and
forbearance are also unequalled. The ingenuity of custom mount maker David
LaTouche and his team solved the numerous challenges that arose in preparing and
mounting the show. Ann Antoshak, graphic designer for both the exhibition and
catalogue, brought together visual materials and text in unusually distinctive ways,
bringing to the project a wonderful combination of playfulness and elegance. Special
thanks also goes to Frank Baseman, who designed the public relations brochure and
family gallery guide; Tamara Block and Anton Stayduhar of Contour Woodworking;
Carl Guckleberger and his team of art handlers; and J. S. Cornell and Son, whose
staff and subcontractors were intimately involved in the practical work of building
cases and outfitting the exhibition spaces.

Two of the institutions that have loaned us objects from their collections deserve
a special note of thanks for collaborating with us: the Museum of Comparative Zoology
of Harvard University (along with the Harvard Museums of Natural History) and
the Academy of Natural Sciences of Philadelphia. At Harvard I wish to thank Directors
Joshua Basseches and James Hanken, along with Karsten Hartel, Constance Rinaldo,
Dana Fisher, and especially Douglas Causey, who coordinated the loans and generously
offered specimens from the ornithology collection that had not been shown in
Philosophical Hall since Charles Willson Peale closed his museum there in the
early-nineteenth century. I am greatly in Harvard's debt for entrusting the specimens
to the Society and to Doug for the many hours he cheerfully devoted to addressing
the complicated issues such a loan required.

At the Academy of Natural Sciences of Philadelphia (ANSP), I thank Director
James Baker whose generosity in agreeing to the loan of more than forty objects
made his institution a real collaborator on the project. Robert McCracken Peck,
Academy Librarian and Senior Fellow, has not only served as an author in this
catalogue but facilitated every aspect of our work at his institution. His dedication
to the project as a friend and colleague is deeply appreciated. Former librarian
C. Danial Elliott and Archivist Earle Spamer have been extraordinarily generous
in providing manuscript materials and books that greatly enhance the exhibition.
Other staff members in the research and curatorial departments at the Academy
have nurtured our investigations and endured our many visits to the collections with
understanding and good cheer. At the risk of omitting some ANSP staff members
who have worked behind the scenes and who will, I hope, forgive my not mentioning
all their names, I owe special thanks to Ted Daeschler, Ned Gilmore, Richard McCourt,
Nate Rice, and Mark Sabaj.

Other colleagues whose institutions have loaned us objects and whose cooperation has been exceptional include Judith A. Warnement of the Harvard University Botany Libraries, Donald Pfister and Lisa DeCesare at the Harvard Herbaria; Michael Ryan, Nancy M. Shawcross, and Lynne Farrington at the Walter S. and Leonore Annenberg Library of Rare Books and Manuscripts at the University of Pennsylvania; John Van Horne and James Green at the Library Company of Philadelphia; Janet Evans at the Horticultural Society of Pennsylvania; John Dann and Brian Dunningan at the William L. Clements Library of the University of Michigan; and Charles E. Pierce, Jr. and Kathleen Stuart at The Morgan Library.

Finally, to friends and family who have been hearing about natural history for many months and providing invaluable moral support, I offer my sincere thanks and love.

SUE ANN PRINCE
Curator and Director of the Exhibition

Author Biographies

Joyce Elizabeth Chaplin is a Professor in the Department of History at Harvard University. She holds a B.A. degree in American culture and psychology from Northwestern University, and M.A. and Ph.D. degrees in history from the Johns Hopkins University. Her most recent book is *Subject Matter: Technology, the Body, and Science on the Anglo-American Frontier, 1500–1676*, and her current scholarship includes nature in eighteenth-century British America and book-length studies of Benjamin Franklin's science. She is currently co-editor of the Johns Hopkins monograph series, *Early America: History, Context, Culture*.

Michael Gaudio is an Assistant Professor of art history at the University of Minnesota. He holds a B.A. in English from the University of North Carolina, a M.A. in art history from the University of Kansas, and a Ph.D. in art history from Stanford University, with a dissertation titled *America in the Making: John White and the Ethnographic Image*. A recent article, "Swallowing the Evidence: William Bartram and the Limits of Enlightenment," was published in the Winterthur Portfolio. He has also served as editor of the *Stanford Humanities Review*.

Robert McCracken Peck has been a Fellow of the Academy of Natural Sciences of Philadelphia since 1983. He is now Academy Librarian and Senior Fellow. He holds a B.A. from Princeton University and a M.A. from the Winterthur Program in American Cultural History, University of Delaware. Widely published, Mr. Peck is the author of *Land of the Eagle: A Natural History of North America*, the companion volume to the eight-part BBC/PBS television series of the same title. It was named one of the ten most notable natural history/science books of the year by *The New York Times Book Review*. He has curated exhibitions not only at the Academy, but also at the American Museum of Natural History, and the University of Pennsylvania Museum.

List of Illustrations

Color Plates

Black and White Figures

Stuffing Birds, Pressing Plants, Shaping Knowledge

Natural History in North America, 1730–1860

DRACONTIUM *fœtidum*

SUE ANN PRINCE

Stuffing Birds, Pressing Plants, Shaping Knowledge

Natural History in North America, 1730–1860

Introduction

"Natural history" is a curious term. Neither "natural" nor essentially "historical," it is both a concept and a practice: a concept that until recently held that nature could be contained and organized into grand, fixed schemes, and a practice that has entailed everything from stuffing birds and pressing plants to comparing bones and painting pictures. Perhaps more important, natural history has always been grounded in the belief that humans can understand and attain dominion over nature by naming, labeling, organizing, and theorizing about its endless manifestations.

The exhibition *Stuffing Birds, Pressing Plants, Shaping Knowledge: Natural History in North America, 1730–1860* explores the cultural assumptions that governed the practice of natural history on the North American continent in the eighteenth and early nineteenth centuries. Focusing on the study of living things— the plant and animal kingdoms—it looks at how and why Euro-Americans of the Enlightenment and post-Enlightenment periods went about explaining the world in the way they did.

OPPOSITE Pierre Jean François Turpin, *Skunk Cabbage (Symplocarpus foetidus) ("Dracontium fatidum")*, n.d. Watercolor, graphite, and ink. American Philosophical Society.

Believing in an inherent order in nature and in the ability of humans to discern that order, European and American naturalists attempted to name, classify, and systematize all natural things. In the process, they created elaborate, artificial systems in order to make sense of what was, and still is, an uncontainable and untidy natural world. Most of the early Enlightenment systems, whether based on arbitrary features or on actual relationships among living organisms, were developed according to visible, external characteristics such as the stamens and pistils of flowers. Later, by the nineteenth century, systems were being developed according to such criteria as invisible and internal functions, anatomical structures, and environmental forces. No matter how elaborate these intellectual "information systems" became, they were too rigid to encompass nature's effusive diversity. Human ordering and natural variety were not a perfect fit because phenomena such as extinction and change were difficult to accommodate.

By examining concepts of nature in the eighteenth and early nineteenth centuries, the exhibition offers perspectives on what constituted knowledge at the time. It also acknowledges other ways of understanding the natural world by revealing "nature" as a concept that changes over time and across cultures rather than as a knowable, "natural" thing. The displays present the systematics of Enlightenment natural history, for example, through manuscripts and books such as the 1735 *Systema Naturae* of Swedish botanist Carl von Linné (Linnaeus) and the Native American language vocabularies compiled by naturalist-statesman Thomas Jefferson. Both men attempted to organize and compare selected attributes of their objects of study.

But the exhibition simultaneously presents specimens in a way that counters the very premises of such systematic orderings. Unlike the hierarchical arrangements that Charles Willson Peale used in his late eighteenth- and early nineteenth-century natural history museum in Philadelphia's Philosophical Hall—also the site of the current exhibition—the specimens are arranged more in keeping with the principles of sixteenth- and seventeenth-century cabinets of curiosity (PLATE 1 AND FIGURE 2).[1] In such cabinets, aesthetically inspiring arrangements were used to create a sense of awe and wonder by stimulating the senses as well as the mind—without regard for an object's place in a presumed natural order. Neither systematics nor cabinets of curiosity tell the whole story.

The remarkable period covered by the exhibition saw the final flowering of the Enlightenment mode of natural history before it was fractured into more specialized scientific disciplines such as zoology, botany, astronomy, geology, and ethnography.[2] Thus, the naturalists whose works are on display were still polymaths with broad interests and talents. William Bartram, for example, had the skills to survive a four-year, 2,400-mile expedition in the Florida wilderness where he not only had to protect himself from snakes and alligators, but also had to negotiate with the American Indians whose territory he was intruding. Simultaneously, he made some of the most beautiful drawings of plants produced in North America at the time, and he wrote about his experiences in a book published in 1791. Titled *Travels in North and South Carolina, Georgia, East and West Florida,* it was a remarkable and innovative mix of travel writing, scientific description, and poetic outpourings. The Scottish-American Alexander Wilson not only taught school but shot birds, eviscerated them, stuffed them, taught himself to draw and paint them, and marketed his nine-volume book *American Ornithology.*

The decision to focus on the period in modern natural history when the study of nature was systematized but not yet compartmentalized into modern-day disciplines was intentional. It presented an opportunity to highlight some of the most spectacular collections at the American Philosophical Society and to present a few of the rare extant specimens that were displayed in Philosophical Hall more than two hundred years ago when Peale's museum was located there. Simultaneously it allowed for an in-depth exploration of early natural history practices in North America and an opportunity to reflect upon how that period's understanding of nature still influences our own.

As a backdrop for North American natural history, books and manuscripts of European *philosophes* are presented, beginning with the innovative taxonomies of Linnaeus and the iconoclastic notions of variation and utility purported by Georges Louis Leclerc, comte de Buffon. Following the texts of these first-generation *philosophes* are the works of other well-known philosopher-naturalists such as Antoine-Laurent de Jussieu, Baron Georges Cuvier, Etienne Geoffroy Saint-Hilaire, and J. B. P. A. de Monet de Lamarck. The European systematics section ends with Charles Darwin's original hand-written title page for *On the Origin of Species,* the book about evolution and natural selection that challenged all earlier explanations of nature, including the fixity of species and the "great chain of being."

Building on the work of the European *philosophes,* the exhibition moves to its primary focus: naturalists working on the west side of the Atlantic Ocean, people who often but not always followed the theories that migrated here from abroad. Indeed, all Euro-American naturalists in the exhibition—Mark Catesby, Cadwallader Colden, William Bartram, Benjamin Smith Barton, C. S. Rafinesque, Alexander Wilson, John James Audubon, Asa Gray, and Louis Agassiz, among others—had to come to terms with European Enlightenment thought. Some of them concurred with its principles or at least attempted to work within its various systems. Others refuted them.

One curious challenge to European theories was embodied in a widespread belief in swallow submersion: the idea that swallows hibernated under water during the winter rather than migrating south. Based on testimonials by apparently credible people who attested to seeing the birds go under water and emerge in the spring, bird submersion theories proliferated. They were founded on the presumed veracity of anecdotal observation without regard for the birds' lack of ability to survive underwater. Even after two men, one a member of the American Philosophical Society, performed an experiment in the Schuylkill River at Philadelphia that resulted in the drowning of two swallows, many naturalists insisted upon the credibility of reported observations of swallow submersion.[3] The tenacity of this position reveals a widespread acceptance of the truth of "facts" based on first-person accounts—a methodology that was self-consciously developed at least in part to distinguish American natural history from the theoretical and systematic bent of its European counterpart.[4]

That counterpart—the Enlightenment-based systematics as practiced on the Continent and revealed through books and manuscripts in the exhibition—usually entailed a representation of nature through hierarchical schemes constructed by naturalist-philosophers as a means of ordering and classifying all of nature's manifestations. The exhibition also presents specimens, which stand in for living objects in a very different way. Indeed, a specimen is a curious means of representing nature because what is used—whether a skeleton, a skin, or a dried flower—is composed of all or part of what was the living thing itself. It is thus more than a representation but less than real, live nature. It is mediated by human hands, whether in the form of a bone removed from the context of a body, a skin stuffed with straw, or a flattened flower deprived of fluid and color. Yet specimens were universally used for study and as "live models" for drawings and paintings.

Robert Peck, in his essays "Preserving Nature for Study and Display" and "Alcohol and Arsenic, Pepper and Pitch: Brief Histories of Preservation Techniques," discusses the many intriguing ways that animals and plants were preserved and prepared for exhibition. Wine, rum, gin, brandy, and other spirits were a favorite for fleshy specimens but so were substances such as cinnamon, tobacco dust, ground pepper, and arsenic. Most of the literature on taxidermy came from Europe, but Charles Willson Peale was among the first to use arsenic to keep insects away from his mounted displays. Peck also explores other fascinating practices, from the cleaning of crustaceans by ants to the drying and varnishing of fish skins.

The impact of preservation techniques on the study of specimens has rarely been addressed. Artworks—drawings, watercolors, and engravings, which constitute at least one-half of the exhibition—are more easily accepted as objects that mediate our experience of nature. Included in the displays are images that reveal not only the beauty and uniqueness of natural objects, but also the various visual conventions that were used to represent them. One such convention, perhaps used unconsciously, was the projection of human qualities onto nature, as can be seen in the uncanny but doleful eye and near smile of a bison created by Mark Catesby (PLATE 9). Another was the frequent transformation of a natural object into an unnatural, stylized, artistic form, as in John Edwards Holbrook's transfiguration of a snake in the wild into a striking abstract form on a white page.

Indeed, as Michael Gaudio discusses in his essay, "Surface and Depth: The Art of Early American Natural History," early naturalist-artists were not mere transcribers of nature. They vacillated between the "dream of [their] imagination," to use the words of Sir Francis Bacon, and a "pattern of the world."[5] Many of the images in the exhibition reveal such a tension between the object portrayed and the artistic imagination behind it—despite the naturalist-artists' frequent claims of objectivity. Breathtaking in their beauty and variety, the drawings and watercolors on view also reveal many a fascinating story about North American natural history.

Finally, the exhibition addresses the popularization of natural history, a concept and mode of thought that was as timely to people two hundred years ago as ecology and environmental science are to us today. Other sections bring to life the influence of natural history on literature, and outdated notions such as a belief in the "fascinating faculty" of the rattlesnake—its presumed ability to cast a spell on its prey.[6]

It is difficult for us to imagine the awe felt by Colonial naturalists when they arrived from the Old World and experienced a vast continent still little explored by Europeans. They were greeted by a plethora of flora and fauna that differed from what they had known at home: plants that devoured insects, snakes that rattled, bones indicating the presence of huge mysterious mammals, and dark reddish peoples living in tribal communities. The opportunity to see, describe, and classify such phenomena in writing, often for the first time, was intoxicating.

Yet naturalists on this side of the Atlantic lived in circumstances quite different from their colleagues in the Old World; few structures were in place to support their work, and few amenities were available for their use. Books, equipment, and funding had to come mostly from abroad until well into the nineteenth century. Indeed, nearly all naturalists who worked in North America, whether Europeans who came to explore and then leave for home, or colonists who were here to stay and become Americans, were supported by patrons in Europe hungry for both information and specimens from the New World. Thus, it is not surprising that most Euro-Americans took their lead from the European *philosophes*—even though they did not always agree with them—rather than from the indigenous peoples already occupying the land. In general the Euro-Americans turned to Native Americans only for help in negotiating the wilderness or for information on the medicinal properties of plants.

Despite the frustrating delays in communication between Europe and America, the naturalists here exchanged information regularly with those abroad and sent them an astonishing number of specimens, from lizards, snakes, butterflies, and sea shells to skunk cabbages and ferns—as well as drawings and written descriptions. British patrons such as London apothecary James Petiver collected the specimens he received and others such as Peter Collinson and John Fothergill made gardens out of them; Linnaeus and others added New World discoveries to their taxonomic systems. In exchange, the Euro-American explorers received patronage and sought but did not always receive respect from Enlightenment centers such as Paris and London.

In her essay "Nature and Nation: Natural History in Context," Joyce Chaplin addresses the conflict between the universal qualities of nature and the national interests of the people studying it. Chaplin focuses on the differences between Britain, where major contributions to natural history served as a foundation for imperial power, and the United States, where natural history practices after the Revolutionary War emphasized the uniqueness of North American nature as a means of gaining credibility in the eyes of the world. Thus, on both sides of the Atlantic, argues Chaplin, knowledge about nature was inflected by national interests.

Natural history was indeed a national pursuit in America. Charles Willson Peale noted in a text for a lecture that "it ought to become a NATIONAL CONCERN, since it is a NATIONAL GOOD."[7] Peale, like many others, linked the climate of freedom in the new country to its potential for leadership in science. Among the many other extant documents that reveal how naturalists in North America viewed their role is a lecture given to the Philadelphia Linnaean Society in 1807 by botanist Benjamin Smith Barton. In his talk, Barton aimed to encourage and inspire young naturalists who were members of the Society. Many of them practiced medicine as did Barton. For most of them, the study of nature was a passionate avocation but not their primary field of endeavor. Barton conveyed his own excitement about natural history, extolling its importance in his introduction:

> Natural History, Gentlemen, is the object of our institution
> [Philadelphia Linnaean Society]. This is a field so extensive, and with
> respect to this country, so interesting and so new, that none of us,

whether our object be the usefulness which attends, or the fame
which follows science, need extend our inquiries far beyond its limits.[8]

He then spoke of the "higher charms" of natural history—its "just and happy
arrangements" and its "beautiful and correct theories. . . ."[9] His words endorsed the
world view of Linnaeus. At the end of his talk, Barton called the audience to action
even more forcefully, invoking Linnaeus as a model, despite an acknowledgment of
some problems in the latter's taxonomic systems:

> I am far from being a blind idolater at the shrine of Linnaeus. I am
> not ignorant of the imperfections of his systems. . . . But these errors
> . . . are few in number.—And in regard to his Systems, should they
> *all* (as some of them, unquestionably, will) crumble into dust, or
> share the fate of other systems, neglect,—the world, a thousand years
> hence, will continue to regard, with veneration and with wonder,
> those powerful and successful efforts, which called Natural History
> from an embryo and misshapen state into form, into regularity, and
> beauty, and even placed it in one of the most elevated stations among
> the sciences which have attracted the notice of mankind, during
> the whole of the eighteenth, and the first years of the nineteenth,
> century. . . . Let us follow, I say, the footsteps of the great modern
> architect of natural history.[10]

In the body of the talk Barton offered a definition of natural history and set
forth the state of the field as he saw it in 1807. Noting that Pliny the Elder and other
Romans had considered it the study of all physical knowledge, including astronomy
and geography, Barton claimed that it had a much more limited scope in the early
nineteenth century. Struggling to define it decisively, he concluded that it referred
to "the Physical History of Nature on this Globe." He immediately qualified his own
definition, however, by claiming that his phrase was too extensive, noting that natural
history did not encompass such fields as "anatomy, physiology, chemistry, *materia
medica*, the history of light and colours, or that of the tides."[11] Clarifying even further,
he organized natural history into six different fields: zoology, botany, geology,
mineralogy, hydrography, and meteorology.[12] This was an early enunciation of some
of the specializations that would develop later in the century.

Among the many other topics Barton summarized and recommended for further study was an investigation of swallow migration (to refute the notion of swallow submersion); a continuing exploration of the extinct mastodons; and further study of the mysterious *crotalus horridus* and other rattlesnakes, creatures that both fascinated and frightened most naturalists. His long discussion of these and other issues in natural history, in a paper that came to seventy-four pages when published, offers an important glimpse into the status quo of North American natural history at the midway point of the period explored in both the exhibition and this catalogue.

The essays that follow offer insights into the preservation of scientific specimens, the art of visual representation, and the intellectual and historical grounding of eighteenth- and early nineteenth-century natural history. By exploring the underlying scientific, visual, and philosophical structures that governed the study, collection, and representation of living things during the Colonial period and early republic, they offer a splendid opportunity to look at natural history from three different perspectives.

In summary, natural history was highly influential in shaping how Europeans and Euro-Americans of the period made sense of their world. Just as the Internet structures the way many of us access and organize information today, the systems and representations created by naturalists shaped the way many people at the time went about understanding life on earth. More specifically, in North America, the work of naturalists not only informed early European-Americans' understanding of nature, but also participated in transforming a whole continent into a Euro-American world.

Endnotes

1. Peale's entire museum was in Philosophical Hall from 1794 until 1802, at which time the majority of objects were transferred to the Long Room in the State House (now Independence Hall). The "Mammoth Room" remained in Philosophical Hall perhaps until 1822.

2. The exhibition and catalogue address the natural history of living things only, leaving aside the natural history of the earth and the sky (now geology and astronomy).

3. Andrew Lewis, in Chapter 1 of his dissertation, documents the belief in swallow submersion, citing numerous examples. He claims that the theory was "one of the most actively discussed and frequently recurring natural history subjects in print and oral culture." Lewis, "The Curious and the Learned: Natural History in the Early American Republic" (Yale University, 2001), 20. I have drawn primarily on his work in my discussion.

4. Lewis, Chapter 1, especially 31–48.

5. Gaudio cites Bacon in the first paragraph of his essay. See also his endnote 1.

6. See Benjamin Smith Barton, "A Memoir Concerning the Fascinating Faculty which has been Ascribed to the Rattle-Snake, and Other American Serpents" in *Transactions of the American Philosophical Society, held at Philadelphia, for Promoting Useful Knowledge*, vol. IV (Philadelphia: Printed by Thomas Dobs): 72–113.

7. Charles Willson Peale, "Introduction to a Course of Lectures on Natural History, Delivered in the University of Pennsylvania," Nov. 16, 1799 (Philadelphia, 1800), 10-12.

8. Benjamin Smith Barton, *A Discourse on some of the Principal Desiderata in Natural History, and on the Best Means of Promoting the Study of this Science in the United States*, a lecture presented to the Linnaean Society of Philadelphia on 10 June 1807 (Philadelphia: Printed by Denham & Town, 1807), 10.

9. Barton, *Discourse*, 12.

10. Barton, *Discourse*, 72–73.

11. Barton, *Discourse*, 12.

12. Barton, *Discourse*, 13.

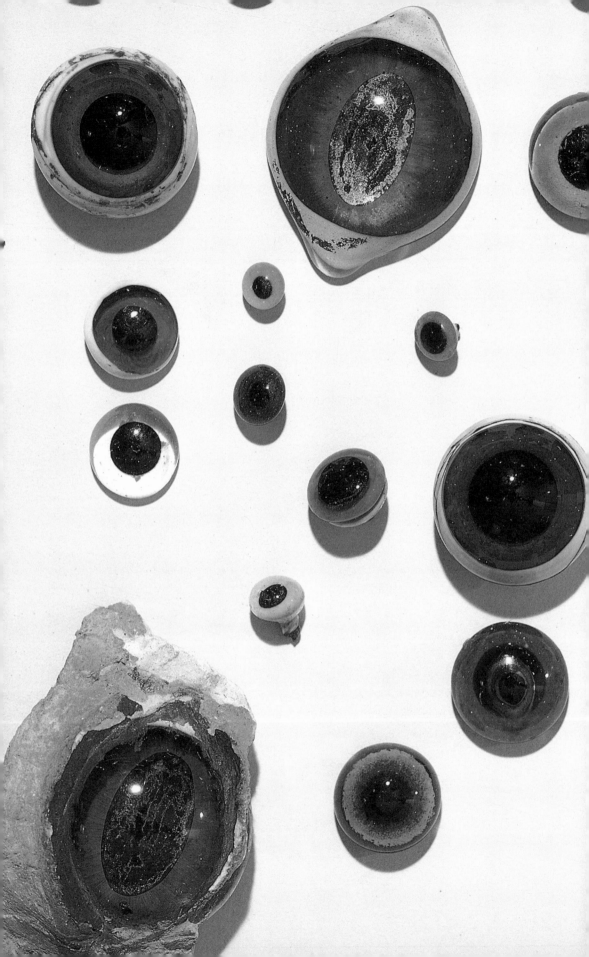

ROBERT McCRACKEN PECK

Preserving Nature for Study and Display

Since at least the sixteenth century, with the establishment of the first quasi-public natural history collections in Europe,[1] naturalists of the Western world have devoted considerable time, energy, and material resources to collecting and preserving wild organisms for study. Despite biblical admonitions against laying up treasures on earth, "where moth and rust doth corrupt,"[2] such efforts were usually justified, at least in part, as a way of honoring and celebrating Divine creation, as if laying up treasures *of* the earth was inherently different than laying up treasures *from* it.

In 1790, the Philadelphia artist, naturalist, and collector of natural history speci-mens Charles Willson Peale issued a broadside in which he described his desire to create a "repository of valuable [natural history] rarities" that might one day "grow into a great national museum." He expressed the hope that, among other things, his display of specimens would increase "knowledge in the works of the Creator," thus bringing the visiting public "nearer to the Great-First-Cause."[3]

Four years later, at the invitation of the American Philosophical Society, Peale moved his fast-growing museum from an outbuilding at his home at Third and

OPPOSITE, DETAIL OF FIGURE 3   Maker unknown, *Glass Eyes (some hand-painted) for taxidermy*, ca. 19th C. The Academy of Natural Sciences of Philadelphia.

Lombard Streets to Philosophical Hall. He then issued another broadside in which he tried to stimulate support for his efforts by heralding both the religious and practical benefits of his growing collection:

> Mr. Peale Flatters himself with a continuance of the public
> patronage, persuaded that his fellow citizens are fully sensible how
> much science and virtue go hand in hand; how the contemplation
> of the marvelous works of God exalts the soul . . . , inspires congenial
> goodness, and [encourages] that love of order so indispensable to
> public and private prosperity.[4]

Peale's English contemporary, George Humphrey, a commercial dealer in natural history specimens, offered a very similar melding of religious and secular justifications for his activities in a manuscript handbook that detailed techniques for acquiring and preserving the creations of nature:

> Enquiries into the Works of the Great Author of all Things are
> praise-worthy as they not only afford a rational Amusement
> to ourselves but are frequently productive of Good to our fellow
> Creatures. . . . The making collections of natural bodies . . .
> at the same time they increase the general Stock of Knowledge,
> contribute greatly to the Recreation of our Friends.[5]

Once the philosophical tenets for their collecting were established and any religious objections overcome, the greatest challenge facing collectors was how to protect their objects from the prophesied "corruption" of moths, rust, and other agents of decay. The earliest techniques for preserving and preparing specimens were developed in isolation or shared through personal contact between individual collectors. A more public (published) exchange on the subject was not begun until the middle of the eighteenth century.[6]

It was clear from the start that shells, insects, minerals, fossils, plants, and other products of the natural world each required different methods of preservation. Large vertebrates, such as birds, fish, and mammals, provided a greater challenge, but for this reason, they were often considered the most desirable part of a serious collection. They also were popular for display in public houses. One such establishment, which flourished in Chelsea (London) from 1695 to 1799, boasted so many natural history speci-

FIGURE 1 Edward Donovan,
*Instructions for Collecting
and Preserving Various
Subjects of Natural History. . . .*
London: Privately printed,
1794. Plate 1, Figure 1.
The Academy of Natural
Sciences of Philadelphia.
Photograph by Will Brown.

PRESERVING NATURE FOR STUDY AND DISPLAY

mens that it was known locally as the "Museum Coffee House" or the "Chelsea Knackatory."[7] Noted by Benjamin Franklin as a sight worth seeing, this popular attraction listed among the 293 rarities in its 1732 catalogue, a starved cat found between the walls of Westminster Abbey, a pair of garter snakes from South Carolina, a 15-inch-long frog, a giant's tooth, barnacles, petrified rain (whatever that was), and "a whale's pizzle."[8] Like other establishments of its kind, it also contained a liberal assemblage of stuffed birds and mammals that were lost to insects, replaced, and lost again several times during the coffee house's century-long run.

From the late seventeenth century on, most serious collectors agreed that the best way to protect fleshy specimens from the damaging effects of air, dust, mold, insects, and other corrupting agents was to immerse them in wine, rum, gin, brandy, or other more generic "spirits."[9] While reasonably effective, this technique presented a number of practical challenges, and the resulting specimens were less than appealing to the eye. More often, collectors—and the public—preferred dry specimens to be displayed as free-standing sculptures. As preservatives grew more toxic and the need to protect

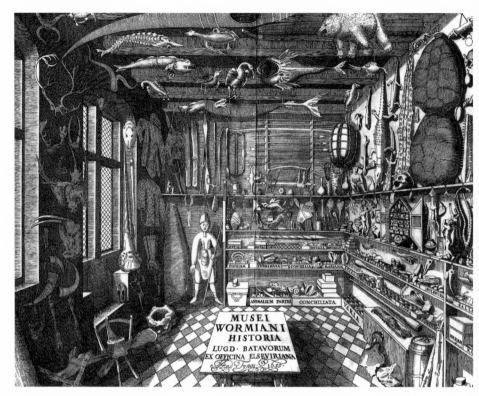

FIGURE 2 Artist unknown, *Museum Wormianum seu Historia rerum rariorum, tam naturalium, quam artificialium, tam domesticarum, quam exoticarum quae Hafniae danorum in aedibus authoris servantur.* Leiden: Elsevier, 1655. Private collection. Photograph by Rosamond W. Purcell.

specimens from the environment became better understood, these were put under glass domes or encased in sealed glass shadow boxes.

The fashion of displaying mounted mammal heads on the wall, which grew from a much earlier European tradition of exhibiting trophy antlers and horns, began in the early nineteenth century and reached the height of popularity in the Victorian era. In the United States, Thomas Jefferson was among the first prominent figures to display both traditional antler "racks" and mounted heads in his home. In a letter to Charles Willson Peale of September 1807, the president thanked his friend for "dressing the Argali head for me."[10] Unfortunately, like so many other mounted mammals, birds, and fish from this period, Jefferson's big-horn sheep head no longer exists (although a replica of it still hangs in the front hall at Monticello).[11]

Recent x-rays of the oldest surviving taxidermic specimen—an African grey parrot buried in Westminster Abbey with its owner in 1702—reveal that, although the bird was gutted, its skeleton, brain, tongue, and windpipe were left intact.[12] This appears to have been common in the earliest preparations. As preservation techniques improved in the eighteenth century, however, the specimens of birds and other large vertebrates more often were prepared with their internal organs and skeletal structure removed.[13] After all remaining flesh and fatty tissue was cut away, skins were usually washed in water, treated with an alcohol solution, and dried (sometimes in an oven). As part of the drying process, various combinations of spices and chemicals were applied to the skin to discourage subsequent insect infestation. The most favored eighteenth-century insecticides included tobacco dust and ground pepper. As a complement to these, George Humphrey recommended the use of "corrosive sublimate [mercurous chloride], flowers of Sulphere, musk, cinnamon and other spices, tansy, wormwood, scotch snuff, camphire, hops, and powdered tar or pitch."[14] Another eighteenth-century English preparer, Edward Donovan, suggested many of the same herbs and spices, but he also included burnt alum, tanners' bark, and arsenic on his list of ingredients for insect-proofing mounted skins.[15] In a letter published by the Royal Society in 1771, a third practitioner suggested first applying a liquid varnish of turpentine and camphor, then dusting the skin with corrosive sublimate, saltpeter, alum, flowers of sulphur, musk, black pepper, and coarsely ground tobacco.[16]

Once a skin had been treated with one or more of these spices and chemicals, it was considered stable and ready for mounting. A wooden or metal armature was usually created to give structure to the creature before it was filled with stuffing (FIGURE 1). Straw, cotton, wool, oakum, hemp fiber (called tow), wood fiber (sometimes called "wood wool"), and chopped flax were the materials generally employed to "flesh out" or plump up the empty skin. Wax or glass eyes were inserted, and if the mouth was to be displayed in an open position, teeth made of bone or porcelain were installed, along with a sculpted tongue. Sutures of cotton thread, sinew, or fine wire closed the original dissecting cuts and completed the process.

Many of the earliest mounted specimens of birds, fish, and mammals, as illustrated in seventeenth-century engravings, have the appearance of bloated pinata dolls suspended from the ceilings of their collector's "cabinets" (FIGURE 2). Other specimens appear to have shrunk and twisted to become grotesque caricatures of their former selves.

Because the most commonly used chemical deterrents to mice, rats, moths, der-mestid beetles, and a host of other flesh-eating scavengers were only partially effective, specimens that were preserved before the end of the eighteenth century in any way other than by immersion in alcohol rarely survived for more than a few decades. In a 1770 critique of contemporary preparation techniques, T. S. Kuckahn described the

usually deteriorated condition of bird specimens treated with raw alum, salt, and
pepper: "They never fail to become humid in moist air and long continued wet weather,
suffer the flesh to rot and even corrode the wires made use of to consine the birds
to their natural attitudes, till the whole drops to pieces on the least touch or motion."[17]

Using the preservation techniques of their English and European contemporaries
and their predecessors, American collectors found their specimens vulnerable to the
same deterioration and loss. Charles Willson Peale resolved that by building on exist-
ing knowledge in the field, he would work to develop a more effective way to safeguard
his collections. If his museum was to represent both the work of the Creator and the
unique fauna of the United States, he reasoned, and if it was to justify his own investment and that of the public (through government grants), he would have to find a way
to safeguard it for posterity. Thus, before formally launching his enterprise, he began
to experiment with techniques for repelling insects from his displays.

The first chemical formula effectively to protect bird and mammal specimens
from insect attack was created in the 1770s by the French apothecary Jean-Baptiste
Bécoeur, but he kept his preservation technique secret in hopes of profiting from the
discovery.[18] Drawing upon a French treatise on taxidermy loaned to him by Benjamin
Franklin[19] and extrapolating from what other information he could find, Peale developed his own successful treatment in 1788. As part of a 1792 promotional campaign,
Peale proudly recounted his achievement in the third person:

> His labours herein have been great and disappointments many,
> especially respecting proper methods of preserving dead animals
> from the ravages of moths and worms. In vain he hath sought, from
> men, information of the effectual methods used in foreign countries;
> and after experiencing the most promising ways recommended
> in such books as he has read, they proved ineffectual to prevent
> depredations by the vermin of America. But, in making various
> other experiments, he at length discovered a method of preservation
> which he is persuaded will prove effectual. . . .[20]

While others were still trying to preserve specimens with a combination of heat, tobacco
dust, and ground pepper, Peale was rendering his skins insect proof by immersing
them in arsenic and hot water.[21] It was a technique he would continue to refine and
improve as new information became available.[22]

As important as Peale's arsenic treatment was in extending the life of his mounted specimens (most of which were ultimately destroyed by fire, not insects), his greatest contribution to museum display may have been his theatrical use of rocks, vegetation, and painted backgrounds to create realistic habitat groups for his specimens.[23] The 140 glass-fronted displays that Peale created for his museum are clearly visible in his famous self-portrait, "The Artist in His Museum" of 1822 (PLATE 1).

Adding to the realism of his installations was Peale's ability to create the illusion of skeletal structure and musculature in his birds and mammals. He did this by mounting his skins on anatomically accurate wooden forms. Earlier taxidermists had used wooden frames or wire armatures to support the general shape of their subjects, but their techniques could not approach the life-like fidelity of Peale's method. "It is a faithful imitation [of the muscles in living animals] made at the expense of great labour," he wrote, "and requires much skill in carving them well, yet for Objects meant to be permanent and faithful, it is all important."[24] Peale's technique would not be used again until the early twentieth century, when the American artists Carl Akeley and James Lippitt Clark developed a similar sculptural approach to taxidermy.[25]

In his earliest mounts, Peale used wax to represent the eyes he had removed.[26] Later, to increase the life-like appearance of his specimens, Peale used glass eyes. This was a technique commonly used in England and Europe in the late eighteenth century as indicated by Edward Donovan in his *Instructions for Collecting and Preserving Various Subjects of Natural History* (1794):

> The eyes are made of glass, and may be purchased at the glass bead
> manufactories, of any size or colour; black are those which suit most
> subjects, but if it should be necessary to have only a black or dark
> speck in the centre of a white bead, it can be blown with a pipe to a
> proper size on the bead or painted with oil colour.[27]

Donovan's subsequent comment that "to prevent obstacles, it will be most advisable for travellers to purchase a complete assortment [of glass eyes]," suggests that by the last decade of the eighteenth century, taxidermy was widely practiced in such urban centers as London and Paris (FIGURE 3).

Peale's technique for mounting skins on carved wooden forms was one of two notable exceptions to the universal practice of stuffing a skin with straw, cotton, or chopped flax. The other was developed by the eccentric English explorer and naturalist Charles Waterton, who visited Peale's museum, and discussed mounting techniques with his son Titian Ramsay Peale, during a trip to North America in 1824.

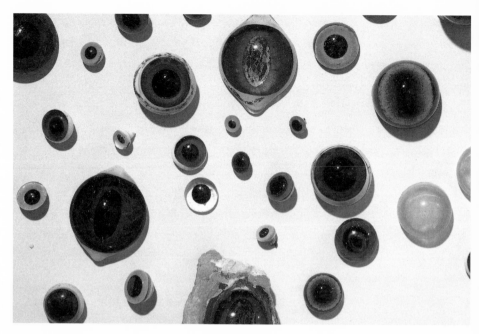

FIGURE 3   Maker unknown, *Glass Eyes (some hand-painted) for taxidermy*, ca. 19th C. The Academy of Natural Sciences of Philadelphia.

So renowned was Waterton for his taxidermy, that Charles Willson Peale used the occasion to paint his portrait—complete with a mounted bird and the severed head of a cat—for display in Peale's own museum[28] (PLATE 2).

Given the hospitality they had shown him, Peale's family must have been somewhat taken aback when they subsequently read Waterton's severe criticism of taxidermied specimens in the world's museums including, one presumes, their own. "It may be said with great truth," wrote Waterton, "that, from Rome to Russia, and from Orkney to Africa, there is not to be found, in any cabinet of natural history, one single quadruped which has been stuffed, or prepared, or mounted (as the French term it) upon scientific principles. Hence, every specimen throughout the whole of them must be wrong at every point.[29]

The year following his Philadelphia visit, Waterton published a detailed account of his own unique approach to curing skins and mounting them without the use of any internal supporting structure. He used the occasion to attack all other methods as leading to "deformity, distortion, and disproportion."[30] Waterton was a strong believer in the power of "spirit of turpentine" and "corrosive sublimate in paste" to fend off insect pests. He expressed his "strong conviction that the *arsenetical soap* can never be used with any success, if you wish to restore the true form and figure of a skin."[31]

The time, expense, and artistic talent required for Waterton's approach to taxidermy was considerable (he took seven weeks to prepare one specimen of a peacock), but the results were impressive. Many of the life-like specimens he created during the first decades of the nineteenth century—including some humorous composites—are still in excellent condition and on view at the museum in Wakefield, West Yorkshire. Along with Charles Willson Peale's few remaining specimens (now at the Museum of Comparative Zoology, Harvard University, PLATE 3), they are among the oldest and best preserved taxidermied specimens in the world.

Charles Waterton prided himself on having collected and mounted most (if not all) of the specimens in his private, and very personal, museum. His satirical mounts often served as three dimensional statements of his political views while the rest served as souvenirs of his South American "wanderings." Peale, by contrast, sought to create a more comprehensive collection, or what he called "an Epitome of the World, where the various interesting subjects of every country may be brought into one view."[32] For this reason, like Ulisse Aldrovandi, the voracious seventeenth-century Italian collector to whom he often compared himself, Peale sought to expand his collections by gift or exchange from as many people and from as many parts of the world as he could arrange.[33]

Some of Peale's earliest specimens came from famous friends and supporters such as Benjamin Franklin, who gave him a dead Angora cat, and George Washington, who presented a pair of golden pheasants that he had been given by the Marquis de Lafayette (PLATE 4). Many others were obtained from collectors whose names have long since been forgotten.[34] When Peale's sons Rembrandt and Rubens traveled to Europe in 1802 to display one of two mastodon skeletons excavated by their father, they were charged with obtaining new specimens for the museum—and with replacing old ones that had been lost to the constant predation of insects: "It is necessary that I inform you," wrote the elder Peale to his son Rubens, "that of the list of European Birds [on display in the museum] which you have, some of them are totally destroyed by dermest [beetles] & I wish others to replace them."[35]

With the popularity of natural history study then exploding in England and throughout the Continent, the young Peale brothers found abundant opportunities for specimen acquisition. "A very good collection of Curiosities might be bought in London," Rubens wrote his father from the British capital. "Preserved Birds and beasts are in windows all over the Town."[36] They also were to be found in many private collections. All that was needed to secure the desired items was cash or specimens of equal value to trade. "I wish you to send anything you please, it is no matter how common," pleaded Rubens: "Birds, Quadrupeds, Fish, Snakes (in spirits), Insects, Shells, Oysters, Clams, Mussels, &c."

The Peale brothers were particularly impressed by a large collection of specimens and drawings of insects from North America that they examined within a few weeks of their arrival in London:

> A Mr. Francillon has the finest collection in Europe of Insects,
> from the southern States of America, on Saturday the 6th we began
> the examination of this collection which consists of Insects from
> different parts, amounting to 7000 Specimens, classically arranged.
> The colours were superior to anything I ever beheld, Fifteen folio
> volumes of drawings of the *worm*, the *crysalis*, and the *fly*, with the
> Plants which they feed on, besides several hundred not bound. The
> drawings and a part were exicuted by a [s]Chool Master in Georgia
> whose name I do not recollect, also the Insects from Georgia &c.
> This collection I understant he has for sale the price of which
> is 2000 pounds Sterling or 8,888 Dollars which is moderate.[37]

While Peale did not buy the insect specimens from Georgia (probably collected by John Abbot), he did collect and prominently display thousands of insects in his museum.[38] Entomology was a field of particular interest to Peale who, in 1795, noted in his diary: "Some collectors like myself have only looked for subjects large and striking to the sight— but now I declare I find an equal pleasure in seeking for an acquaintance with these little animals who[se] life is spent perhaps on a single leaf or at most on a single *bush*."[39]

Peale's personal interests and biases in natural history did not always translate proportionally to the exhibits in his museum. Because his was a commercial as well as a scientific venture, some subjects (e.g. birds, minerals, and fossil bones) were given more space and prominence than others, such as plants—a group of organisms that did not easily lend themselves to public display, except as live specimens in botanical gardens and arboreta. They were of considerable interest to botanists, horticulturists, and physicians, however, and so were actively exchanged internationally. One has only to think of the mutiny on the Bounty (1789), with its cast off crates of living breadfruit trees, to be reminded how much importance was given to the acquisition of new plant species by private collectors and governments alike.

The correspondence of collectors and naturalists in the seventeenth, eighteenth, and early nineteenth centuries is rife with references to plants being sent from one part of the world to another. In North America, plants were among the first natural resources described and collected. Pressed specimens of America's flora were proudly added to European herbaria, where many remain today. After independence, and as the United States government acquired more land and pushed its borders westward, scientists continued to expand their inventory of native plants and animals. Lewis and Clark, Stephen Harriman Long, and Zebulon Pike were among the first to receive government support for their collecting activities.

When these explorers left on their historic journeys to explore America's western frontier, they carried essentially the same requests for information and instructions for collecting and preserving specimens that had been offered to travelers for more than three centuries. James Petiver, Edward Donovan, William Curtis, George Humphrey, William Swainson, Abel Ingpen, Charles Willson Peale,[40] and every other natural history collector from the start of the Renaissance to the present day has instructed others to handle specimens with reverence, but to collect them with abandon. In 1696 the antiquarian and geologist John Woodward urged travelers to "neglect not any[thing], tho' the most ordinary and trivial: the Commonest peble or Flint, Cockle or Oyster-shell, Grass, Moss, Fern, or Thistle, will be as useful . . . as any the rarest production of the Country."[41] One hundred sixty-seven years later, a collectors' guide issued by the Academy of Natural Sciences of Philadelphia gave much the same advice: ". . . we would here recommend you not to be deterred from bringing any object from the circumstance of its being 'very common;' but would rather advise you to preserve every natural curiosity that you may meet with."[42]

Some have viewed mankind's quest to collect and preserve the world's flora and fauna with humor (PLATE 5), but most westerners have seen it as a useful enterprise closely tied to the moral, social, intellectual, and material advancement of individuals, institutions, and nations. In the late eighteenth century, France so valued the natural history collections of William V of Holland that they treated them as trophies of war and transported them by the tens of thousands to the museum in Paris.[43] Today, although natural history specimens are seldom targeted by warring nations, they are considered important parts of each nation's patrimony. What the founders of the Academy of Natural Sciences of Philadelphia had to say about specimens almost two centuries ago still is relevant today:

> Natural History can only be studied by means of natural objects; and in order to render the latter useful, they must be carefully exhibited, arranged and labelled. To effect these important ends requires the cooperation of many individuals, together with much time, labour, and scientific knowledge.[44]

Endnotes

1. Among the most important early nonprincely collections were those assembled by the Swiss naturalist Conrad Gesner, the Italian collector Ulisse Aldrovandi in Bologna, and the Danish professor of medicine Ole Worm in Copenhagen. For more on these and other early collections see Oliver Impey and Arthur MacGregor, eds., *The Origins of Museums: The Cabinet of Curiosities in Sixteenth and Seventeenth Century Europe* (Oxford: Clarendon Press, 1985). See also Silvio A. Bedini, "The Evolution of Science Museums," *Technology and Culture* 6 (1965): 1–29.

2. Gospel according to St. Matthew 6:19.

3. Charles Willson Peale, Broadside (Feb. 1, 1790), quoted in Charles Coleman Sellers, *Mr. Peale's Museum: Charles Willson Peale and the First Popular Museum of Natural Science and Art* (New York: W.W. Norton & Co., 1980), 45–47.

4. Charles Willson Peale, Broadside (Sept. 19, 1794), quoted in Lillian B. Miller, ed., *The Selected Papers of Charles Willson Peale* (New Haven: Yale University Press, 1988), 98. All references to Miller are drawn from volume 2, parts 1 and 2, of this important series; pages are numbered sequentially.

5. George Humphrey, manuscript handbook entitled *Collecting and Preserving all kinds of Natural Curiosities* (1776), Coll. 371, Archives, Academy of Natural Sciences of Philadelphia.

6. Important early publications in methods of preserving natural history specimens include: R.A.F. Réaumur, "Diverse means of preserving from corruption dead birds, intended to be sent to remote countries, so that they may arrive there in good condition," *Philosophical Transactions*, 45 (1748): 304–320; E. T. Turgot, *Mémoire instructif de réassembler, de préparer, de conserver et d'envoyer, les diverses curiosités d'histoire naturelle* (Paris & Lyon: J. M. Bruyset, 1758); J. R. Forster, *A catalogue of the animals of north America . . . to which are added short directions for collecting, preserving, and transporting all kinds of natural history curiosities* (London: White, 1771); Letters by British artillery captain lieutenant Thomas Davis (March 12, 1770) and by T. S. Kuckahn of London (written between May 22 and July 5, 1770), *Philosophical Transactions* LX (1771): 184–187 and 302–320; and A. Manesse, *Traité sur la manière d'empailler et de conserver les animaux, les pelleteries et les laines* (Paris: Guillot, 1787). All these authors were cited frequently in subsequent publications.

7. A. Stuart Mason, *George Edwards: The Bedell and his Birds* (London: Royal College of Physicians, 1992), 28–29.

8. Richard D. Altick, *The Shows of London* (Cambridge, MA: Harvard University Press, 1978), 18.

9. Among the earliest practitioners of this form of preservation was a collector named Robert Boyle who experimented with preserving a linnet in alcohol in 1663. By 1689, W. Charleton was recommending brandy as the best preservative, in W. Charleton, *Onomasticon* (London, 1668). Both are cited in R. T. Gunther, *Early Science in Oxford* (Oxford: Oxford University Press, 1925), 104–105. See also Wilma George, "Alive or Dead: Zoological Collections in the Seventeenth Century," in Oliver Impey and Arthur MacGregor, eds., *The Origins of Museums* (Oxford: Clarendon Press, 1985), 184.

10. Letter from Thomas Jefferson to C. W. Peale (Sept. 24, 1807), quoted in Miller, 1029–1031.

11. The original head, almost certainly a specimen collected by Lewis and Clark, was transferred to the University of Virginia following the president's death. It has been missing since the 1870s. Donald D. Jackson, ed., *Letters of the Lewis and Clark Expedition with Related Documents, 1783–1854* (Urbana: University of Illinois Press, 1962) 2, 734.

12. P. Morris, "The Antiquity of the Duchess of Richmond's Parrot," *Museums Journal* 81 (1981): 153–154.

13. The parrot, which once belonged to the Duchess of Richmond, is now on display in the museum at Westminster Abbey. For a discussion of early taxidermy techniques, see Christopher Frost, *A History of British Taxidermy* (Lavenham, Suffolk: privately printed, 1987).

14. Humphrey, 5.

15. Edward Donovan, *Instructions for Collecting and Preserving Various Subjects of Natural History* (London: privately printed, 1794), 2–4. An anonymous author offers similar advice in *The Naturalist's and Traveller's Companion Containing Instructions for Discovering and Preserving Objects of Natural History* (London: George Pearch, 1772).

16. *Philosophical Transactions* LX (London: The Royal Society, 1771): 312.

17. *Philosophical Transactions* LX, 304.

18. Barbara and Richard Mearns, *The Bird Collectors* (San Diego: Academic Press, 1998), 43.

19. The treatise had been given to Franklin in July 1773 by Louis Marie Jean Daubenton, one of Buffon's collaborators on the great *Histoire naturelle*. Peale copied "Directions for preserving Birds &c." into his letter book in 1787. See Sellers, 24.

20. C. W. Peale, "To the Citizens of the United States of America," *Dunlap's American Daily Advertiser* (Jan. 13, 1792), quoted in Miller, 9–10. Miller says that this advertisement was run repeatedly throughout 1792. Sellers says that it first appeared as a broadside and advertisement in January 1790. See Sellers, 45–46.

21. Peale further protected his specimens (in this case from human damage) by prominently placing signs around the gallery that read "Do not touch the birds as they are covered with arsenic Poison." See William T. Alderson, ed., *Mermaids, Mummies, and Mastodons: the Emergence of the American Museum* (Washington, D.C.: American Association of Museums, 1992), 26.

22. When Bécoeur's formula for arsenical soap was eventually disseminated by curators at the natural history museum in Paris, Peale was quick to adopt it. See Letter from C. W. Peale to Stephen Elliott (Feb. 14, 1809), quoted in Miller, 1180–1181.

23. A decade after Peale had pioneered the concept of habitat displays in Philadelphia, the British impresario William Bullock developed similar exhibitions in his natural history museum in London. See Richard D. Altick, *The Shows of London* (Cambridge, MA: Harvard University Press, 1978), 237. The British collector E. T. Booth (1840–1890) further developed such display techniques in his private museum in Brighton in the second half of the nineteenth century. See P. A. Morris, "An Historical Review of Bird Taxidermy in Britain," *Archives of Natural History* 20, Part 2 (1993)2: 248–249.

24. Letter from C. W. Peale to Stephen Elliott (Feb. 14, 1809), quoted in Miller, 1988, 1179. Peale sometimes called upon the wood sculptor William Rush to assist him with this work.

25. For a discussion of their techniques in taxidermy, and a good history of diorama-making, see Karen Wonders, *Habitat Dioramas: Illusions of Wilderness in Museums of Natural History* (Uppsala, Sweden: Acta Universitatis Upsaliensis, 1993). See also Penelope Bordry-Sanders, *Carl Akeley: Africa's Collector, Africa's Savior* (New York: Paragon House, 1991).

26. Humphrey also suggested using "pitch or black sealing wax" for this purpose, while Thomas Davis, who wrote "A Method of Preparing Birds for Preservations" in 1770, suggested that eyes could be replicated "by dropping drops of black sealing wax on a card of the size of the natural ones." *Philosophical Transactions* LX (1771): 186.

27. Donovan, 3.

28. The portrait is now in the collection of the National Portrait Gallery, London.

29. Charles Waterton, *Essays on Natural History* (London: Longman, Brown, Green and Longmans, 1837), 322.

30. Like T. S. Kuckahn, he favored the use of "corrosive sublimate" (mercurous chloride) and turpentine. His detailed instructions for preserving and mounting birds is contained in *Wanderings in South America* (London: J. Mawman & Co., 1825). See p. 304 for quotation cited here. Waterton presented a copy to Titian Ramsay Peale, who heavily annotated the section entitled "On Preserving Birds For Cabinets of Natural History." Peale's copy of Waterton's book

is in the Ewell Sale Stewart Library of the Academy of Natural Sciences. For a discussion of Waterton's technique, see Christopher Frost and Brian Edginton, *Charles Waterton A Biography* (Cambridge: The Lutterworth Press, 1996).

31. Charles Waterton, *Essays on Natural History*, (London: Longman, Brown, Green, and Longmans, 1844), 74, 76, 78.

32. Charles W. Peale to the American Philosophical Society (March 7, 1797), quoted in Miller, 177.

33. Peale was so enamored of Aldrovandi that in October 1795 he named one of his sons in his honor. Some months later, probably on the suggestion of his wife and with the enthusiastic encouragement of the American Philosophical Society (on whose property the child had been born), he renamed his son in honor of Benjamin Franklin. See Miller, 177–178, and Sellers, 88.

34. Within a few years of opening his museum, Peale had developed an international network of exchange that resulted in an exponential growth of his collections. By moving his museum first to Philosophical Hall and then parts of it to the State House, he created the opportunity for continued expansion. For a discussion of some of Peale's donors, see David R. Brigham, *Public Culture in the Early Republic: Peale's Museum and its Audience* (Washington, D.C.: Smithsonian Institution Press, 1995).

35. Charles W. Peale to Rubens Peale (Aug. 30, 1802), quoted in Miller, 451. Presumably, these lost specimens had been acquired by Peale already mounted and thus did not have the protection of Peale's arsenical preservative.

36. Rubens Peale to Charles W. Peale (Sept. 6, 1802), quoted in Miller, 455.

37. Rubens Peale to Charles W. Peale (Sept. 23, 1802), quoted in Miller, 458.

38. According to Sellers, Peale had some 4,000 insects on view in the museum between 1804 and 1810. See Sellers, 162. Peale did subsequently purchase some bird specimens from Abbot. See Miller, 861. For more about Abbot's collections, see Virginia Rogers-Price, *John Abbot in Georgia: The Vision of a Naturalist Artist (1751–ca. 1840)* (Madison, GA: Madison-Morgan Cultural Center, 1983).

39. Charles Willson Peale, *Diary* (1795), 10–11, Peale Papers, American Philosophical Society; also quoted in Sellers, 87, and in Miller, 121.

40. For a typical letter from Peale offering suggestions on what to collect and how to preserve it, see his letter to Messrs. Fanning and Coles (June 6, 1808), Peale Papers, American Philosophical Society, quoted in Sellers, 201.

41. John Woodward, quoted in Arthur MacGregor, "The Cabinet of Curiosities in Seventeenth-Century Britain," in Impey and McGregor, 155–156.

42. *Circular*, pamphlet issued by the Academy of Natural Sciences of Philadelphia (1829): 2.

43. In 1795 the French, who had recently invaded Holland, laid claim to the natural history collections of Stadholder William V. The first shipment to the Paris Museum, comprising about half of the collection, was packed in ninety-five boxes and consisted of 10,000 specimens of minerals, 3,872 botanical specimens, 5,000 insects, 9,800 shells, and 1,176 bird specimens. See Florence F. J. M. Pieters, "Notes on the Menagerie and Zoological Cabinet of Stadholder William V of Holland, Directed by Aernout Vosmaer," *Journal of the Society for the Bibliography of Natural History* 9, part 4 (April 1980): 541–542.

44. *Circular*, 2.

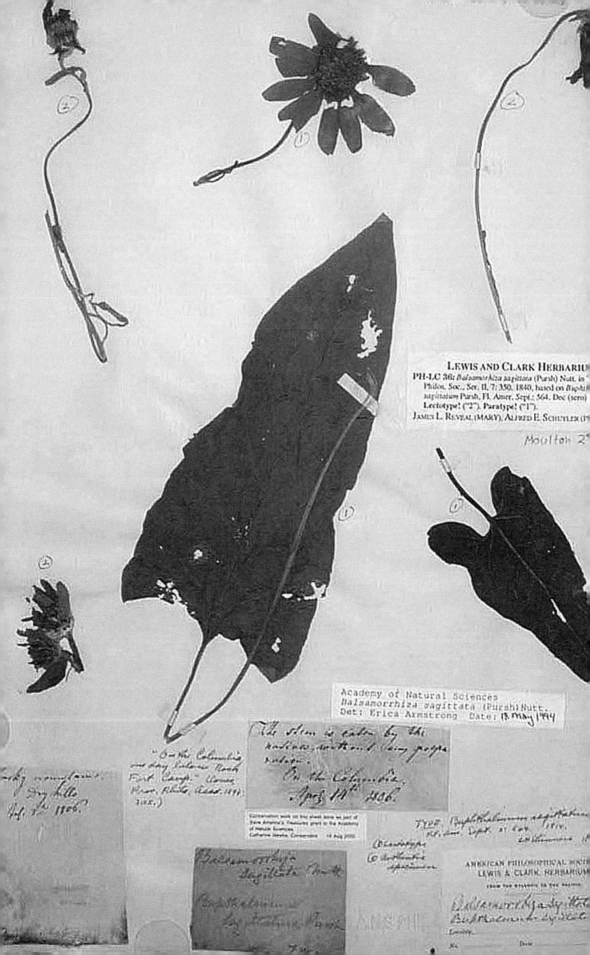

Academy of Natural Sciences
Balsamorhiza sagittata (Pursh) Nutt.
Det: Erica Armstrong   Date: 18 May 1994

Alcohol and Arsenic, Pepper and Pitch

Brief Histories of Preservation Techniques

Insects | *Drowned in Spirits, Stuck with Pins*

When the great Swiss encyclopedist Conrad Gesner attempted to bring together all that was known about the animal kingdom in his massive *Historia Animalium* (1551–1558), he found insects to be a group about which there was already so much to say that he needed to publish a separate monograph on the subject. His untimely death prevented his doing so, but three quarters of a century later, with additions from at least two other authors, his manuscript was published as Thomas Moffet's *Insectorum Theatrum* (1634).[1] The number of exotic insects described and illustrated in this pioneering work, and in other entomological publications of the seventeenth, eighteenth, and nineteenth centuries, attests to the extent to which foreign insects, including many from the Americas, were available to natural history enthusiasts in Europe and Great Britain through trade and purchase.[2]

OPPOSITE, DETAIL OF FIGURE 11 Meriwether Lewis and William Clark, *Arrowleaf Balsamroot (Balsamorhiza Sagittata)*. Two specimens collected by Lewis in Lewis and Clark Pass, Montana, July 7, 1806, and by Clark along the Columbia River in Skamania or Klickitat County, Washington, April 14, 1806. American Philosophical Society, on deposit at the Academy of Natural Sciences of Philadelphia.

Insects were an ideal subject for study because, unlike birds and mammals, they were conspicuous, abundant, universally distributed, and relatively easy to collect. They could be raised in captivity or preserved and transported anywhere in the world with ease. Because of the small size and modest cost of most insects, even scholars of limited means and with finite space for storage and display could create significant collections.

The London apothecary James Petiver, who amassed an enormous collection of insects and other natural history specimens at the end of the seventeenth century, relied on a network of sympathetic friends and associates to provide him with "whatever plants, shells, insects, &c they shall meet with, preserving them according to directions that I have made so easy as the meanest capacity is able to perform."[3]

Petiver's instructions for preserving insects were relatively simple. He said:

> Butterflies must be put into your Pocket-Book, or any other small printed book as soon as caught, after the same manner as you dry plants. [Beetles] may be Drowned altogether as soon as caught in a little wide-mouth'd Glass or Vial of the aforesaid Spirits or Pickkel, which you may carry in your pocket.[4]

In addition to a copy of his printed instruction manual, Petiver often supplied his correspondents with collecting nets, insect traps, paper, pins, jars, and "preserving liquor."[5] For a German naturalist planning to collect for him in Maryland in 1698, Petiver even sent a personal assistant, a boy he called "my Butterflie Catcher," who was charged with drowning in spirits all "Flies, Beetles, Caterpillars, & other Insects especially such as you shall find in water" and pressing between the leaves of a collecting book "Butterflies & Moths of each of wch get al you can find."[6]

Sadly, many of Petiver's insects were subsequently lost due to poor preservation, poor storage conditions, and poor handling.[7] Miraculously, another eighteenth-century insect collection, assembled by William Hunter, has survived to the present day almost entirely intact. It was given to Glasgow University in 1781, where it is still housed in its original cabinets with its original labels.[8] Other eighteenth-century collections can be seen in the Zoological Museum at the University of Copenhagen, the Natural History Museum in Paris, the Natural History Museum at the University of Uppsala, the Oxford University Museum of Natural History, the Zoological Museum at Kiel University, the Natural History Museum (formerly the British Museum [Natural History]) in London, and at the Macleay Museum at the University of Sydney in Australia.

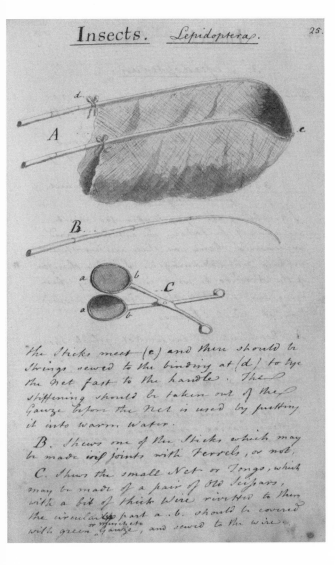

Although American insects collected in the seventeenth and eighteenth centuries
are contained in a number of English and European collections, no collections of
comparable age survive in North America. Thomas Say, the Philadelphia naturalist
who is often called the "father of American entomology," may have amassed the largest
American collection of insects prior to 1850, but many of his specimens, like those
of James Petiver, were lost due to poor preservation and careless handling in the years
immediately following the collector's death.[9] Say, who understood better than anyone
the constant attention required of an insect collection, despaired when specimens
being sent to him from Europe were delayed in transit. "The detention of boxes of
insects, I need not say, is their destruction," he observed.[10] While Say did not publish

FIGURE 5 Titian Ramsay Peale, *Butterfly Box* (disassembled). The Academy of Natural Sciences of Philadelphia. Photograph by Will Brown.

his own techniques for collecting or preserving insects, his correspondence and a heavily annotated book on English insects from his library, now at the Academy of Natural Sciences, suggest that he was probably using techniques employed by most of his contemporaries.[11]

Most entomologists of the eighteenth century used the equipment described and illustrated by George Humphrey in his hand-written instruction book for traveling collectors (1776) (FIGURE 4) and in other works such as *The Naturalist's and Travellers Companion* by W. Curtis (1772) and *Instructions for Collecting and Preserving Various Subjects of Natural History* by Edward Donovan (1794). According to Donovan, the typical eighteenth-century kit included: "A large Bat-Fowling-net, a pair of forceps, a number of corked boxes of various sizes, ditto small pill boxes, a spare box with clamps and a pincushion well stored with pins of different sizes."[12]

"When in search of insects," instructed W. Curtis, "we should have a box suitable to carry in the pocket, lined with cork at the bottom and top to stick them upon, until they are brought home. If the box be strongly impregnated with camphor, the insects soon become stupefied and are thereby prevented from fluttering and injuring their plumage." He continued:

> In hot climates insects of every kind, but particularly the larger, are
> liable to be eaten by ants and other small insects, especially before
> they are perfectly dry: to avoid this, the piece of cork on which our
> insects are stuck in order to be dried, should be suspended from the
> ceiling of a room, by means of a slender string or thread, besmear
> this thread with bird-lime . . . to intercept the rapacious vermin. . . .[13]
> After our insects are properly dried, they may be placed in the cabinet
> or boxes where they are to remain: . . . the bottoms of the boxes
> should be covered with pitch, or green wax, over which paper may
> be laid, or, which is better, lined with cork, well impregnated with
> a solution of a quarter of an ounce of corrosive sublimate mercury,
> in half that quantity of aetherial oil of turpentine, and a pint of the
> camphorated spirit of wine.[14]

In the nineteenth century, more and more specialized equipment was recommended for insect collectors. The English naturalist Abel Ingpen offered several pages of descriptive text and two color plates on collecting, rearing, and preserving equipment in his widely distributed *Instructions for Collecting Insects, Crustacea and Shells* (1839) (PLATE 6). In another instruction manual published the following year, William Swainson offered a similar list of collecting tools that he considered essential for professionals and amateurs alike. For securing insects alive, he suggested collectors should have "phials, chip boxes, and breeding cages; and for preserving them when dead, pins, braces, pocket boxes, store boxes, and travelling chests."[15]

Once insect specimens were captured, killed, and mounted, Swainson explained, their long-term preservation depended entirely "upon the nature of the boxes that contain them, and the presence of drugs to deter other insects from attacking them."[16] Just as Humphrey had observed more than a half century earlier, Swainson noted:

> In hot climates the ants will find their way to the store boxes of
> the collector in less than an hour, and if the least opening presents
> itself will commence their work of devastation. A box of 200 or
> 300 insects will be destroyed in this way during one night, and
> even before some specimens are quite dead. All insect boxes should

therefore be air-tight; even where ants are not to be feared, the cockroaches will destroy all specimens that may be left exposed during the night.[17]

It was generally recommended that insect specimens be kept either in cork and paper-lined wooden boxes or in wooden cabinets with glazed drawers. Swainson advised collectors that store-bought boxes were more economical, more easily stored and transported, and smaller than their glazed counterparts. "When neatly finished with cloth backs, and labelled," he continued, "the whole may be arranged like books upon shelves, and thus have a very pleasing appearance."[18] The more impressive "glazed drawer" approach to storage required the additional expense of cabinetry. Each custom-made cabinet could hold as many as "forty drawers, arranged in two tiers and protected by folding doors of plain mahogany."[19]

For his father's museum in Philadelphia, Titian Ramsay Peale designed and constructed entomological storage boxes that combined the best features of both designs described by Swainson (PLATE 7 and FIGURE 5). His tinfoil-sealed "book boxes," attractively covered with marbleized paper, could be handled and stored like books but had the display feature of double-glazing. In Peale's boxes, butterflies and moths pinned to small pieces of cork could be viewed from both sides without ever being handled or exposed to light or to the risk of infestation by predatory insects. Inside the covers of each "book," Peale recorded essential information about its contents.

More than 100 butterfly boxes were created by Peale over a forty year period (1828–1870). Given to the Academy of Natural Sciences after the naturalist's death, they constitute the oldest intact insect collection in North America.[20]

While Peale and others who prepared natural history specimens for long-term study and display correctly identified dermestid beetles and rapacious ants as "the worst enemies of the zoological curator," they were quick to recognize that the destructive habits of these insects could be turned to positive advantage.[21] Under controlled conditions, they could be used to remove unwanted flesh not only from skulls and skeletons of vertebrates, but also from the legs, claws, and bodies of large crustaceans.[22]

Eighteenth- and nineteenth-century collecting guides recommended keeping small specimens in spirits, but drying large ones. Several, including those by Donovan and Ingpen, suggested using ants to help. "After they [the crustaceans] are killed," wrote Donovan, "put them into an Ant's nest; those little animals will devour the flesh in a few hours and leave the shell entire."[23]

To prevent decay and to encourage their quick and easy consumption by insect cleaners, crustaceans destined for a museum cabinet first had to be purged of their salty contents. Humphrey recommended doing this by soaking the living specimens in a tub of fresh water, then killing them in "a strong Decoction of Tobacco and fresh water."[24] "Crabs, Lobsters, &c. should on no acct. be put into boiling water," he warned, "as it effectually changes their natural colours and spoils them."[25] Serious collectors, it seems, could not have their crabs and eat them too.

Humphrey called for moderation in preparing crustaceans, noting that they should not be dried by a fire or in the sun because the shells could crack.[26] Other collectors took a more aggressive approach. In his *Instructions for Collecting and Preserving Various Subjects of Natural History* (1794), Donovan recommended "suffocating" crabs in "spirits either of wine or terpentine" and then drying them in an oven.[27]

Eighteenth-century collectors preserved dried crustaceans with tobacco dust, a treatment that deterred but did not completely prevent subsequent insect infestation. Early nineteenth-century collectors used more toxic chemicals. Ingpen suggested stuffing the legs and claws with "cotton dipped in corrosive sublimate" to ward off insect pests.[28] William Bullock, the proprietor of a highly successful museum of natural history in Liverpool and London from 1795–1819, preferred a preservative powder made of arsenic, burnt alum, tanners' bark, camphor, and musk.[29] William Swainson anointed his specimens with "arseniated soap" and urged others to do the same in his 1840 essay "On Preserving Zoological Subjects."[30]

33

ALCOHOL AND ARSENIC, PEPPER AND PITCH

Unlike insects or crustaceans, shells had an appeal that often extended well beyond the realm of the natural history elite. In Renaissance Europe, they were sometimes collected as much for their value and status-raising qualities as for their intrinsic interest as elements of nature. In North America, they were often counted among the most prized components of any natural history collection.

Beginning in the Low Countries in the fifteenth century, shell collecting as a hobby spread quickly throughout Europe.[31] Conrad Gesner, Ulisse Aldrovandi, and Ole Worm each showed a serious interest in acquiring and studying shells. Soon shells drew the attention of Royal collectors, which further enhanced their desirability. In eighteenth-century France, the *Cabinet du Roi* (begun by Louis XIII in 1635) came to exceed all other collections in size.[32] Russia's Peter the Great bought large collections of shells during his visits to Holland. Christian VI of Denmark was a shell collector, as were the kings of Poland and Portugal. In Sweden, King Adolf Frederic and Queen Louisa Ulrica each had shell collections, some of which were examined and described by Linnaeus.[33]

The first book devoted entirely to shells was published at the end of the seventeenth century,[34] but it was not until the middle of the eighteenth century that anyone gave detailed instructions for their collection, preservation, shipment, and display. This may have been because shell collecting was not nearly as challenging as with more fragile organisms. Edward Donovan recommended the use of a fisherman's trawling net, noting that good shells could be acquired after a storm when the "agitation of the water separates them from their native beds." He advised collectors to choose shells that were still under water to avoid faded colors.[35] William Bullock concurred, noting that the best shells "are those that have the living fish in them."[36] George Humphrey, in 1776, advised that shells of "singular shape," with the animal in them, "may be preserved in spirits."[37] The rest he suggested purging of their occupants with scalding water, then drying with care. "Shells must never be placed in the heat of the sun," he warned, "otherwise the colours will fade and the skin with which many of them are covered (and which must on no acct. be taken off) will peal and fly off."[38]

Since Humphrey's instructions were for traveling collectors, he devoted much attention to the best ways to pack and ship shells from one part of the world to another. A few brief excepts from his manual offers practical advice that is still applicable today:

> Such shells whose tips or points are very sharp and tender might
> have them dipped into melted Bees-wax or pitch. . . . A good way to

preserve the small shells is to pack them inside the very large ones, which will also save room. . . . Such shells as are tender should be packed in cotton in small boxes. They should be afterwards packed together . . . in strong boxes which should be close filled up to prevent their shaking & closely nailed down, so to remain till they arrive in England.[39]

Other collectors preferred shipping shells in dry sand, sawdust, or "fine flour."[40] John Lawson, John Banister, Peter Kalm, John and William Bartram, and the many other naturalists who provided American shells to English and European collections used all these techniques when shipping conchological treasures overseas. Once safely deposited in a collector's cabinet, shells were among the most stable of natural history specimens, subject only to environmental degradation over long periods of time.[41]

Unlike shells, whose brilliant colors, beautiful forms, and durable nature made them a desirable ornament for any collector's cabinet, fish were generally collected by only the most curious and ardent naturalists. "The impossibility of preserving the beautiful but evanescent colours of fish," wrote Swainson, "and the unsightly appearances they generally present, whether in spirits or in a dried state, prevents these animals from being much attended to by most scholars."[42] Those who did keep fish for study generally did so either in alcohol or as dried skins.

Despite its tendency to turn specimens a uniform dingy grey color, alcohol was often recommended because it was easy to obtain and effective in preventing decay. It is still the preferred method today. "Very little preparation is necessary for [fish] . . . they are best preserved in spirit of wine, and only require to be washed clean from all slimy matter before they are put into the bottles," wrote Donovan in 1794.[43] Swainson also was emphatic in his recommendation of alcohol as a preservative:

> In preserving fish for the purposes of science, no method is prefer-
> able to that of immersing them in spirits. The mouth, gill, and fins
> can then be spread open; the rays of the one and the internal parts
> of the other can be accurately examined, and even the internal
> structure of the body may be investigated. All these advantages are
> either partially or totally lost to the naturalist when the specimens
> have been either stuffed or dried. . . .[44]

Swainson's admonitions against drying fish not withstanding, this method of preservation was widely practiced in the eighteenth and nineteenth centuries. Swainson recommended that if drying was to be used, a preservative should be applied and the skin "either filled with plaster and attached to a board, or be suffered to dry between leaves of blotting paper and preserved like dried plants."[45] Donovan suggested covering the dried skins with two or three coats of copal varnish.[46]

Collectors interested in public exhibition of their fish usually mounted them on boards or prepared them as life-like sculptures. Charles Willson Peale was especially proud of his fish displays and hoped one day to assemble a comprehensive collection of fishes of the United States, focusing on their economic value to the country.[47] He recommended taking "one side of the fish, and preparing a form in wood then placing the fish on it with the fins extended, and fix the whole on a board, and cover

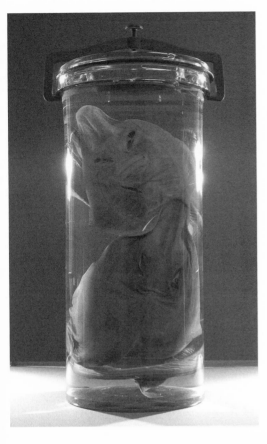

FIGURE 6 Charles Lucien Bonaparte, *Two Common Guitarfish (Rhinobatos rhinobatos)* ("Rhinobatus columnae"). Collected in the Mediterranean Sea near Italy, ca. 1830–1836. The Academy of Natural Sciences of Philadelphia. Photograph by Mark Sabaj.

them with glass to keep them clean."[48] William Bullock developed a secret technique that made the mounted fish in his museum appear to one visitor "so perfect, both as to shape and colour, that they gave the idea of having just been taken out of the water."[49]

Academic naturalists who cared more about details of anatomy than realistic display, generally preferred preserving fish either in alcohol (FIGURE 6) or on paper. In 1745 the German botanist John Frederick Gronovius wrote his Philadelphia friend and American Philosophical Society founding member John Bartram a letter urging that he and the society take on a serious study of fish.[50] To encourage the idea, he sent a copy of the Royal Society's *Philosophical Transactions* that contained an article on classifying and preserving fish. The following year he sent Bartram prescriptions for a "varnish which preserves the fishes" and for a powder "by which any creature, as quadrupeds and birds, are preserved and become very hard." He also sent specimens of fish skins dried and mounted so that they might be "kept as plants in an Herbarium."[51]

Another friend of Gronovius, the Swedish taxonomist Carl Linnaeus, recorded in his autobiography that he kept "in his cupboards innumerable fish glued on paper as

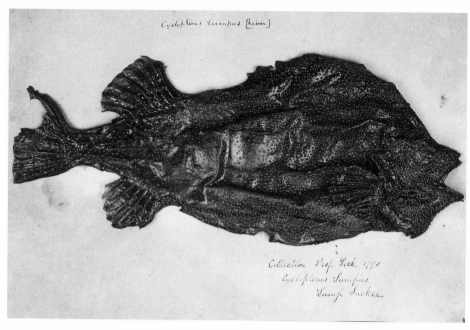

Cycloptous lumpus [him]

Collection Prof. Peck. 1793
Cyclopleus Lumpus
Lump Sucker.

FIGURE 7   William Dandridge Peck, *Lumpsucker or Lumpfish (Cyclopterus lumpus)*. Collected ca. 1793. Museum of Comparative Zoology, Harvard University. Photograph by Mark Sloan.

if they were plants."[52] Some of these had been sent to him from America already dried and mounted on paper by Alexander Garden in 1760.[53] That 168 of Linnaeus' dried specimens still survive is a testament to their preparation and the care given the collection since Linnaeus' death in 1778.

An early American collection using very similar techniques was begun by William Dandridge Peck in 1785.[54] Harvard's first professor of natural history (1805–1822), Peck already had created much of his dried fish collection before seeing other examples in Europe, and thus he either developed the technique himself or based it on correspondence and publications like Donovan's. Between twenty and thirty of Peck's dried fish, which were varnished, then sewn and glued to sheets of paper like herbarium specimens, survive (FIGURE 7). They are the oldest such (dried) specimens in North America.[55]

As contemporary descriptions and catalogues attest, virtually every major natural history collection of the seventeenth and eighteenth century included stuffed crocodiles, alligators, lizards, and snakes as well as the wonderfully sculptural carapaces of turtles and tortoises from around the world.[56]

Specimens of this kind were prepared in much the same way as fish, birds, and mammals. Smaller ones were kept in spirits, whereas larger ones were skinned and treated with preservatives, then either rolled up, stuffed with straw, mounted over a wooden form, or tacked to boards for display. Because of their relatively slow metabolism and long lives, reptiles were sometimes shipped alive from their native habitats and kept in captivity for months or years before being preserved and placed in the more permanent collections of their owners. Snakes were of particular interest to those in the medical profession because of the toxins many were capable of producing.

Rattlesnakes from North America were of interest to an even wider community because of their rumored ability to "charm" their prey and their unusual habit of using their rattles to "warn" potential victims of impending attack. Transatlantic correspondence of the seventeenth and eighteenth centuries is full of requests for rattlesnakes both dead and alive, and many collectors' cabinets of the period boasted American rattlesnake rattles, if not complete specimens.[57]

Beginning in 1682, and running throughout the eighteenth century, reports on rattlesnake behavior and anatomy appeared regularly in the *Philosophical Transactions* of the Royal Society.[58] Through this same period, live specimens were kept—with care— in such places as the garden of the Royal College of Physicians (where Sir Hans Sloane made first-hand observations of their behavior in the spring of 1730).[59] Nor were such creatures of interest only to the *cognoscenti*. An illustrated advertisement in London's *Daily Journal*, placed within weeks of Sir Hans' observations, announced the public exhibition of "two live rattlesnakes just brought from Virginia" as well as the "scarce to be seen Head, Skin, and Rattle of a dead [rattle]snake." These living and dead displays could be seen by anyone for sixpence "at the Virginia Coffee House behind the Royal Exchange."[60]

As transportation improved and knowledge about maintaining wild animals in captivity became more sophisticated, the public display of live snakes and other reptiles grew more common in the late eighteenth and early nineteenth centuries. A visitor to Peale's museum in 1793 reported seeing "an apartment where rattle, black and spotted snakes are confined in cases, enclosed with wire and glass."[61] Peale himself offered the horrified visitor a close look at a five-foot long "black runner," while allowing "the reptile to touch his cheek, and . . . intwine itself round his neck."[62]

Live rattlesnakes, cobras, boa constrictors, crocodiles and alligators, along with exotic birds, mammals, "monsters," and "sea serpents" were regularly featured in traveling menageries in the United States and Europe during the first few decades of the nineteenth century.[63] Some inevitably ended their lives as preserved specimens. An American visitor to Regency London observed a 35 foot long (stuffed) boa constrictor in Bullock's museum in 1811—perhaps a relic of a live animal display. He noted that its extraordinary size "makes the story of Laocoön quite probable."[64]

For serious scholars of natural history, the variety of specimens and the state of their preservation was far more important than their size. In fact, for specimens being preserved in alcohol, small ones were usually preferred; and naturalists traveling to remote areas under conditions in which it was often difficult or impossible to carry large quantities of alcohol usually skinned and dried reptiles rather than using alcohol.

A representative collection of preserved snake skins was assembled by the British naturalist and explorer William Burchell after his 4,500-mile trek through Cape Colony in Southern Africa from 1811 to 1815. Seventy-six have survived to the present day at the natural history museum at Oxford. Burchell's method of preparation began by killing the snakes, cutting them lengthwise, and removing their skeletons and internal organs. The skins were then

> . . . spread out flat on a sheet of strong paper to which the inner-side adhered owing to its own glutinous property. . . . The sheet with the applied snake-skin was then placed between other sheets of absorbent paper so that the moisture in the skin was drawn-off and evaporated. The whole was then put in a press with the head of the snake left out to prevent it being crushed.[65]

William Swainson, while preferring the use of spirits for preserving reptiles and amphibians, acknowledged that skinning might be the only practical way of preparing specimens in the field. He offered advice on doing so in his 1840 handbook that parallelled Burchell's technique quite closely.[66] As for collecting the specimens to begin with, Swainson recommended delegating that duty to "the natives" or "country people who give them provincial names, and who may safely be consulted respecting their habits. Every information on these points the collector will be careful to note among his memorandums."[67]

Burchell, who had no qualms about making his own collections, did acknowledge that no matter how well preserved his specimens were, they were still dangerous: "for death may yet lurk in them, though all life may have left the serpent: not would I give an assurance that even after the lapse of years, the fatal power may not still reside in the desiccated venom. . . ."[68]

Because of their importance as sources of food, clothing, shelter, and medicine, plants have been collected, exchanged, propagated, preserved, described, and illustrated throughout human history. Of all fields of natural history, botany may have the longest tradition of serious study. The oldest surviving institutional herbarium dates from 1545 at the University of Padua in Italy, although a collection of dried plants may have been associated with the botanical garden at the University of Pisa even earlier.[69] Aldrovandi had more than 14,500 specimens and 2,000 illustrations of plants in his own collection by 1570.[70]

While the first half of the eighteenth century saw the establishment of a number of private and institutional plant collections, the publication of Linnaeus' *Species Plantarum* in 1753 greatly expanded academic and popular interest in botany. Some thirty-two institutional herbaria and countless private collections were created in the second half of the eighteenth century.[71] Not surprisingly, this same period saw an extremely active exchange of dried and living specimens from around the world.

In his manuscript guide "Collecting and Preserving all kinds of Natural Curiosities" (1776), Humphrey offered a technique for drying plants that had been practiced for centuries and has remained standard procedure to the present day:

> Specimens of most kinds may be preserved between sheets of whitish brown or coarse brown paper. You must remember to gather them in a dry day, and they should be frequently shifted to fresh paper, and while drying should have a weight on a board laid on them to press them flat.[72]

Donovan suggested that if fresh paper was not available, as was often the case in areas removed from major urban centers, plants could be pressed between the pages of a "large book" instead. Once the plants were dried, he recommended spreading "a thin coat of gum-arabic on the paper" to which the specimens were to be affixed. "They should after this be covered with a thin coat of copal varnish," he continued, "to preserve them from the ravages of insects, or the ill effects of damp."[73]

William Curtis favored keeping his dried plants "either loose in quires of paper, or fastened into a book, with glew made of fine isinglass disolved in boiling water." He further suggested sprinkling "the paper and the stalks of the plants . . . with the sulimate solution," the same insecticide solution with which he treated almost everything else.[74]

The loss of color in dried flowers presented a challenge to botanists who hoped to use this distinctive feature, at least in part, to identify and classify the specimens that were sent to them. To address this deficiency, the Abbe Hauy at the Royal Academy of Sciences in Paris developed an elaborate process of matching leaf and flower parts with pieces of colored paper that he would then cut out to enhance the colors of his faded specimens. In 1785, he presented his unusual technique to the Academy, describing it as follows:

> Of all the productions of nature, there are none more susceptible
> of change than vegetables. . . . Flowers, in particular, soon lose their
> colours in an herbal, and assume others, quite different from those
> bestowed on them by nature. Yellow grows pale, or becomes nearly
> effaced; blue or red are still more apt to fade or disappear entirely . . .
> [They] become, in a few days, so much tarnished, that they cannot
> be known by any eye but that of an experienced botanist. This
> inconvenience I have endeavoured to remedy. . . . For this purpose

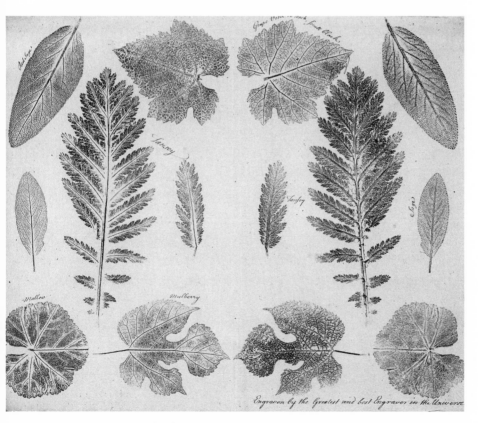

FIGURE 8   Joseph Breintnall, *Book of Leaf Prints*, 1731–1744. The Library Company of Philadelphia.

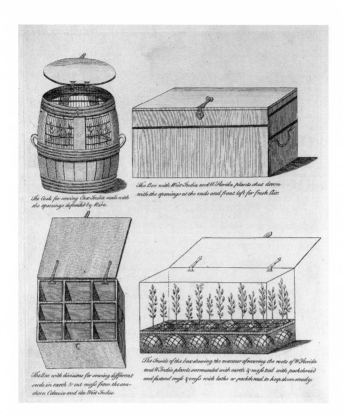

The Cask for sowing East-India seeds with the openings defended by Wire.

The Box with West-India and W.Florida plants shut down with the openings at the ends and front left for fresh Air.

The Box with divisions for sowing different seeds in earth & cut mofs from the southern Colonies and the West-Indies.

The Inside of the box shewing the manner of securing the roots of W.Florida and W.India plants surrounded with earth & mofs tied with packthread and fastend crofs & crofs with laths or packthread to keep them steady.

FIGURE 9 John Ellis, *Directions for Bringing Over Seeds and Plants, from the East-Indies and Other Distant Countries, in a State of Vegetation. . . .* London: L. Davis, 1770. Frontispiece. Pennsylvania Horticultural Society, on deposit at the American Philosophical Society.

I painted a piece of fine paper with water colours in such a manner as to have . . . the same degree of strength as those of nature, only a little fainter. . . . When I had done this, I threw the leaves into spirits of wine, where they soon lost all their colours, and were reduced to whitish transparent membranes. After having dried them thoroughly, . . . I laid them on the coloured paper by means of a thick varnish. . . . I afterwards drew another paper, several times over the flower pressing it strongly with my hand until all the leaves were properly applied, and until the artificial colours appeared through them. . . . I afterwards left the flower a few moments in a press, then, having cut the paper around it, I applied it with a dissolution of gum-arabic to the place it should occupy on the plant, which had been before fixed by means of the same dissolution to a piece of paper of a proper size. . . . I have submitted to the inspection of the academy the Violet and Geranium, and the common Poppy of the fields [prepared in this way], the artificial colours of which have preserved their lustre for many years. . . .[75]

Another interesting approach to plant collecting, which avoided the issue of preservation altogether, was nature printing, a process by which the detailed image of a plant could be transferred to paper. With nature printing the image replaced the fragile plant as the specimen to be kept for future study. The technique, which was first explained and illustrated by Leonardo da Vinci in *Codex Atlanticus* (1490–1505), was recommended to naturalists by Curtis in 1772:

> The impressions of plants well taken off upon paper, look very
> little inferior to the best drawings, and may be done with very little
> trouble. For this purpose, some printer's ink and a pair of printer's
> bosses, such as are used for laying the ink on types, are necessary.
> After rubbing these bosses with a little of the ink, lay the plant
> betwixt them, and press it so as to give it sufficient colour, then take
> the plant and lay it carefully on a sheet of paper, and press it with
> the hand, to give the impression of the plant to the paper, which may
> be afterwards coloured according to nature.[76]

In the 1730s the Philadelphia merchant Joseph Breintnall experimented with the commercial production of nature prints (FIGURE 8). These included sheets recording plants that had been collected for the purpose by John Bartram.[77] A few years later, their mutual friend Benjamin Franklin modified Breintnall's technique and used it to produce some of Pennsylvania's earliest paper currency. A twenty shilling note, bearing the impression of a blackberry leaf, was printed by Franklin in 1739. From then on, because of its attractive appearance and its usefulness in discouraging forgery, nature printing remained an important part of colonial and Continental currency up to and during the American Revolution.[78]

The wealth represented by colonial and postcolonial currency, whether nature-printed or not, played an important part in the exchange of plant material in the seventeenth, eighteenth, and nineteenth centuries. American colonial botanists like John Bartram, while eager to contribute to the growing knowledge of natural history, could not afford to do so without financial subvention. Fortunately, in Bartram's case, an eager group of private collectors in England, led by Peter Collinson and including Charles Lennox, Philip Miller, Lord Petre, Sir Hans Sloane, and others, agreed to support Bartram's efforts.[79] Eventually, King George III allocated a fifty-pound annual stipend to further encourage the collecting of this skilled and knowledgeable botanist. The results were impressive, for Bartram, with the help of his son William, was responsible for introducing almost one-quarter of the 600 American plants in cultivation in Europe at the time of the American Revolution.[80]

One of Bartram's many English customers was the naturalist John Ellis, who wrote, among other things, an influential treatise on shipping seeds and live plants around the globe. Ellis, who undoubtedly followed his own advice when sending tea seeds to Bartram to propagate in 1760,[81] sent a copy of his instructional pamphlet to the Philadelphia botanist at the time of its publication in 1770.[82] The techniques described and illustrated in Ellis' booklet were quickly adopted by collectors throughout the world, and much of his treatise was paraphrased or republished verbatim by other authors, further increasing its impact.

Ellis' procedures were at once simple and ingenious:

> Tea seeds, the stones of mangoes and all hard nuts and leguminous
> seeds, may be pressed by rolling each in a coat of yellow bees wax,
> about half an inch thick; and afterwards a number of these thus
> prepared, may be put into a chip box, which is to be filled with
> melted bees wax, not made too hot: the outside of the box may then
> be washed with the sublimate solution and kept during the passage
> in a cool airy place.[83]

If bees wax was not available, he suggested, "plaster of Paris, mixed with water, and poured upon the nuts, seeds, &c. may be substituted."[84]

Other packing techniques he proposed involved layering seeds between sheets of wax-coated paper, then sealing the entire lot in melted bees wax.

> The small seeds well dried may be mixed with dry sand, put into
> the cerate paper or cotton, and packed in glass bottles, which may be
> covered with a bladder or leather. These bottles may be put into keg,
> box, or any other vessel, filled with four parts of common salt, two
> of saltpetre, and one part of sal armoniac, in order to keep the seeds
> cool and preserve their vegetative power.[85]

Ellis also suggested ways in which seeds could be encouraged to germinate in transit (by packing them in damp moss into which they could "shoot their small tendrils").[86] He offered detailed designs and illustrations for shipping containers in which plants could be safely transported either as seeds or in a vegetative state (FIGURE 9).

Ellis' advice undoubtedly contributed to the successful introduction of hundreds
of new plant species to cultivation during the late eighteenth and early nineteenth
centuries. A surprising number of living specimens from this era of international
exchange can still be found in the botanical gardens of Europe and Great Britain.
An even larger number of dried plant specimens collected during this period have
survived. Many of the North American collections made by John Banister, Mark
Catesby, Peter Kalm, John Bartram, and others can still be seen in British and
European herbaria.

Among the oldest dried plant collections in North America is the *Hortus Siccus*
(literally "dry garden") made by Benjamin Smith Barton, author of the first botanical
textbook published in the United States.[87] As a professor of natural history and
botany at the University of Pennsylvania, beginning in 1789, Barton used his extensive
natural history library, the largest in North America, and his herbarium of native
plants, which also became the nation's largest, to aid in his teaching.[88]

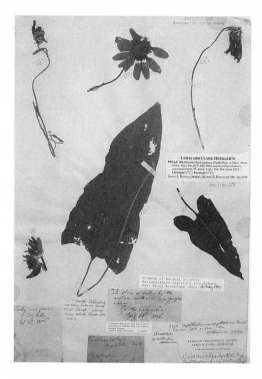

FIGURE 11 Meriwether Lewis and William Clark, *Arrowleaf Balsamroot (Balsamorhiza sagittata)*. Two specimens, collected by Lewis in Lewis and Clark Pass, Montana, July 7, 1806, and by Clark along the Columbia River in Skamania or Klickitat County, Washington, April 14, 1806. American Philosophical Society, on deposit at the Academy of Natural Sciences of Philadelphia.

Because of Barton's particular interest in the medicinal applications of plants (he was named a professor of *materia medica* in 1795), many of the plants he collected have detailed notations concerning their known uses in healing wounds, reducing fevers, or settling upset stomachs. Part of his herbarium is contained in two leather-bound volumes that have protected the plants from the damaging effects of light and mechanical abrasion for more than 200 years. Although some of these specimens have faded or darkened with age, many still appear surprisingly fresh and life-like (FIGURE 10).

Among the long roster of distinguished students to study with Barton was Meriwether Lewis, whom Jefferson sent to Philadelphia for botanical training in 1803, just prior to his historic transcontinental journey to the Pacific coast with William Clark. Although Lewis did not become a botanist during his short period of study, he learned enough about botany to make a number of significant botanical discoveries during his trip. The hundreds of dried plants that Lewis and Clark brought back from their expedition, deposited with the American Philosophical Society by Thomas Jefferson, comprise some of the very first specimens of plants from the American West to come to the attention of the scientific community (FIGURE 11). That they survived the arduous journey and many decades of subsequent mistreatment and neglect is a testament to the way in which they were preserved in the field.[89]

Endnotes

1. S. Peter Dance, *The Art of Natural History* (Woodstock, NY: The Overlook Press, 1978), 29–31. See also Joseph and Nesta Ewan, *John Banister and his Natural History of Virginia, 1678–1692* (Urbana: University of Illinois Press, 1970), 277.

2. It is remarkable how much personal field experience early collectors had in entomology. While the most high-profile student of insects who worked abroad was Dutch artist Maria Sybilla Merian, who distinguished herself by observing and painting live insects in Surinam in the 1690s, there were many others, including the English collector-naturalists John Ray, John Tradescant (who traveled and collected extensively in Europe and North Africa), his son, John Tradescant, Jr. (who made collections in North America in 1637), and Sir Hans Sloane (who published a book in 1696 about his natural history studies in Jamaica from 1687–1692). Other naturalists who focused their attention on this field of study during and after the Enlightenment worked from preserved specimens at home.

3. Quoted in E. St. John Brooks, *Sir Hans Sloane: The Great Collector and His Circle*, (London, 1954), 180–181, and in Arthur MacGregor, "The Cabinet of Curiosities in Seventeenth-Century Britain," in Oliver Impey and Arthur MacGregor, *The Origin of Museums* (Oxford: Clarendon Press, 1985), 156.

4. James Petiver, *Musei Petiveriani* (London 1695), 31, quoted in Wilma George, "Alive or Dead: Zoological Collections in the Seventeenth Century," in Impey and MacGregor, 185.

5. Raymond Phineas Stearns, *Science in the British Colonies of America* (Urbana: University of Illinois Press, 1970), 265, 309, and 346.

6. A transcription of Petiver's instructions to "Issack the Butterfly Boy" is given in Stearns, 272.

7. Petiver's collection was purchased for 4,000 pounds by Sir Hans Sloane in 1714. Sloane's collections were, in turn, purchased by the British government in 1753. They served as the basis for the natural history section of the British Museum. For more on these collections see Brooks,

179–181; Peter J. P. Whitehead, "Museums in the History of Zoology," *Museums Journal* (1971): 50–57 and 155–160; MacGregor, 157; and Richard D. Altick, *The Shows of London* (Cambridge, MA: Harvard University Press, 1978), 15.

8. C. H. Brock, "William Hunter's Museum, Glasgow University," *Journal of the Society for the Bibliography of Natural History* 9 (Part 4): 406. Altick gives the date of Hunter's gift as 1783; Altick, 28.

9. See Patricia Tyson Stroud, *Thomas Say: New World Naturalist* (Philadelphia: University of Pennsylvania Press, 1992), 265–266. In 1993, Jonathan Mawdsley reported that despite the widespread belief that all of Say's specimens had been lost, 770 have survived and are now at the Museum of Comparative Zoology at Harvard University. They are not in their original cases. See Jonathan R. Mawdsley, "The Entomological Collection of Thomas Say," *Psyche* (published by Cambridge Entomological Club) 100, Nos. 3–4 (1993): 163–171.

10. Letter from Thomas Say to Reuben Haines (Feb. 12, 1830), quoted in Stroud, 213.

11. Say's annotated copy of George Samouelle, *The Entomologist's Useful Compendium or An Introduction to the Knowledge of British Insects (With Instructions for Collecting and Putting Up Objects for the Microscope)* (London: Thomas Boys, 1819), was presented to the Academy by his widow, Lucy Say. It is now in the Ewell Sale Stewart Library.

12. Edward Donovan, *Instructions for Collecting and Preserving Various Subjects of Natural History* (London: privately printed, 1794), 22.

13. Humphrey gave almost identical advice; see George Humphrey, manuscript handbook entitled *Collecting and Preserving all Kinds of Natural Curiosities* (1776), Coll. 371, Archives, Academy of Natural Sciences of Philadelphia, p. 29.

14. W. Curtis (?) *The Naturalist's and Traveller's Companion Containing Instructions for Discovering and Preserving Objects of Natural History* (London: George Pearch, 1772), 9–10.

15. William Swainson, *Taxidermy, Bibliography, and Biography* in Dionysius Lardner, ed. *The Cabinet Cyclopaedia* (London: Longman, Orme, Brown, Green, and Longmans, 1840), 8–12.

16. Swainson, 57.

17. Swainson, 57–58.

18. Swainson, 88.

19. Swainson, 90.

20. For a complete description of how and why these book boxes were created, see Titian R. Peale, "Method of Preserving Lepidoptera," *Annual Report of the Board of Regents of the Smithsonian Institution* (1863), 404–406. A 2002 "Save America's Treasures" grant supported the conservation and stabilization of this important collection. I am indebted to Jason D. Weintraub and Catherine A. Hawks for the information they provided about the Peale collection. The Museum of Comparative Zoology at Harvard has more individual insects from the early nineteenth century, but these have been integrated into their entire collection and are not contained in their original cases. See H. A. Hagen, "The

Melsheimer Family and the Melsheimer Collection," *The Canadian Entomologist* XVI (1884): 191–197.

21. Titian Ramsay Peale, "Method of Preserving Lepidoptera," *Annual Report of the Board of Regents of the Smithsonian Institution* (1863): 404.

22. Until the nineteenth century, marine crustaceans were often classified as insects.

23. Donovan, 55.

24. Humphrey, 45.

25. Humphrey, 47.

26. Humphrey, 46.

27. Donovan, 55.

28. Abel Ingpen, *Instructions for Collecting, Rearing, and Preserving British and Foreign Insects: Also for Collecting and Preserving Crustacea and Shells* (London: W. Smith, 1839), 99.

29. For a detailed description of Bullock's museum, see Altick, 235–252. The formula for (and method of) preparing Bullock's preservative powder is given by Swainson, 29.

30. Swainson, 29.

31. For a detailed discussion of the history of shell collecting, see S. Peter Dance, *Shell Collecting: An Illustrated History* (Berkeley: University of California Press, 1966).

32. Henry Coomans, "Conchology Before Linnaeus," in Impey and MacGregor, 191.

33. Coomans, 191.

34. P. Fillipo Buonanni, *Ricreatione dell 'Occhio e Della Mente* (Rome, 1681).

35. Donovan, 59.

36. William Bullock, *A Concise and Easy Method of Preserving Subjects of Natural History, Intended for the Use of Sportsmen, Travellers, etc.* (London, 1817), quoted in Dance, 127.

37. Humphrey, 64.

38. Humphrey, 63.

39. Humphrey, 60–63.

40. George Annesley, *Short Instructions for Collecting Shells* (Bewdley, 1827), quoted in Dance, 129.

41. Shells can be infected by Byne's disease that occurs when acetic and formic acids, released from the wood in some shell cabinets, attacks the shell's calcium carbonate structure. High humidity increases the speed of the chemical reaction.

42. Swainson, 50.

43. Donovan, 9.

44. Swainson, 51.

45. Swainson, 53.

46. Donovan, 9.

47. See various Peale letters in Miller, 745 and 820–821.

48. C. W. Peale, "My Design in Forming This Museum," Broadside (1792), quoted in Miller, 17.

49. Swainson, 51.

50. J. F. Gronovius to John Bartram (April 24, 1745), quoted in Edmund and Dorothy Berkeley, *The Life and Travels of John Bartram* (Tallahassee: University Presses of Florida, 1982), 118.

51. J. F. Gronovius to John Bartram, 2 "Juny" 1746, quoted in William Darlington, *Memorials of John Bartram and Humphrey Marshall*, facsimile of 1849 ed. (New York, 1967), 355, quoted in Berkeley and Berkeley, 118.

52. Quoted in Wilfrid Blunt, *The Complete Naturalist: A Life of Linnaeus* (New York: The Viking Press, 1971), 151.

53. Stearns, 611. See also Alwyne Wheeler, "The Linnean Fish Collections in the Linnean Society of London," *Zoological Journal of the Linnaean Society* 84 (1985): 1–76. For a discussion of the rest of Linnaeus' fish collection, see Fernholm and Wheeler, *Zoological Journal of the Linnaean Society* 78 (1983): 199–286, and Wheeler, *Zoological Journal of the Linnaean Society* 103 (1991): 145–195.

54. *Early Science at Harvard: Innovators and Their Instruments, 1765–1865* (Cambridge, MA: Fogg Art Museum, 1969), 41.

55. For photographs and descriptions of three of Peck's specimens, see David P. Wheatland, *The Apparatus of Science, 1765–1800* (Cambridge, MA: Harvard University, 1968), 190–192.

56. George in Impey and MacGregor, 181. See also Joy Kenseth, *The Age of the Marvelous* (Hanover, NH: Hood Museum of Art, distributed by University of Chicago Press, 1991).

57. George in Impey and MacGregor, 182.

58. See *Philosophical Transactions* XII, No. 144 (Feb. 10, 1682–1683): 25–47; XXXIV, No. 398 (April–June, 1727): 414; XXXV, No. 401, (Jan.–March, 1728): 377–381; XXXVII, No. 433 (July–Aug. 1734): 321–331.

59. Stearns, 291.

60. The original advertisement is in the rare book collection at the Field Museum of Natural History in Chicago. I am grateful to Ben Williams for drawing it to my attention.

61. Miller, 69.

62. Miller, 69.

63. An uncatalogued collection of advertisements for nine-teenth-century live animal displays in England can be seen in the library of the Field Museum of Chicago. See also Altick, and Richard W. Flint, "Entrepreneurial and Cultural Aspects of the Early-Nineteenth-Century Circus and Menagerie Business," *Itinerancy in New England and New York*, Peter Benes, ed., in *Annual Proceedings* of Dublin Seminar for New England Folklife (1984; published by Boston University, 1986), 131–149.

64. Louis Simond, *An American in Regency England* (London, 1968), 139, quoted in Altick, 235.

65. K. C. Davies, "Burchell's Serpents," *Journal of the Society for the Bibliography of Natural History* 9 Part 4 (April 1980): 460.

66. See Swainson, 54–55.

67. Swainson, 6–7.

68. W. J. Burchell, *Travels in the Interior of Southern Africa*, vol. I (London: Longman Hurst, Rees, Orme, Brown and Green, 1822), 471, quoted in Davies, 466.

69. Stanwyn G. Shetler, "The Herbarium: Past, Present, and Future," *Proceedings of the Biological Society of Washington* 82 (Nov. 17, 1969): 695.

70. Paula Findlen, *Possessing Nature: Museums, Collecting, and Scientific Culture in Early Modern Italy* (Berkeley: University of California Press, 1994), 166.

71. For a statistical analysis of the growth of the world's herbaria, see Shetler, 687–758.

72. Humphrey, 113.

73. Donovan, 83.

74. Curtis, 24.

75. Abbe Hauy, quoted by Donovan, 81–83.

76. Curtis, 24–25.

77. Berkeley and Berkeley, 18–21.

78. For a detailed discussion of Benjamin Franklin's role in nature printing, see Eric P. Newman, "Nature Printing on Colonial and Continental Currency," *The Numismatist* 77, Nos. 2, 3, 4, 5 (1964).

79. For a partial list of Bartram's patrons and customers, see Appendix # 6 in Berkeley and Berkeley, 311–318.

80. Joseph Kastner, *A Species of Eternity* (New York: Alfred Knopf, 1977), 49.

81. Berkeley and Berkeley, 192.

82. Bartram was sent a second copy of Ellis' publication by Peter Collinson. See Berkeley and Berkeley, 280.

83. John Ellis, quoted in Curtis, 21.

84. Ellis, 21.

85. Ellis, 22.

86. Ellis, 22–23.

87. Benjamin Smith Barton, *Elements of Botany* (Philadelphia, privately printed, 1803). The oldest plant specimens in North America are those collected by John Bartram, now at the Sutro Library in California.

88. Joseph Ewan, *From Seed to Flower: Philadelphia 1681–1876: A Horticultural Point of View* (Philadelphia: Pennsylvania Horticultural Society, 1976), 49.

89. For a detailed history of the Lewis and Clark specimens, see Gary E. Moulton, *The Journals of the Lewis and Clark Expedition: Herbarium of the Lewis and Clark Expedition*, (Lincoln: University of Nebraska Press, 1999), 12. See also Earle E. Spamer and Richard M. McCourt, "The Lewis and Clark Herbarium of the Academy of Natural Sciences," *Notulae Naturae* 475 (December 2002).

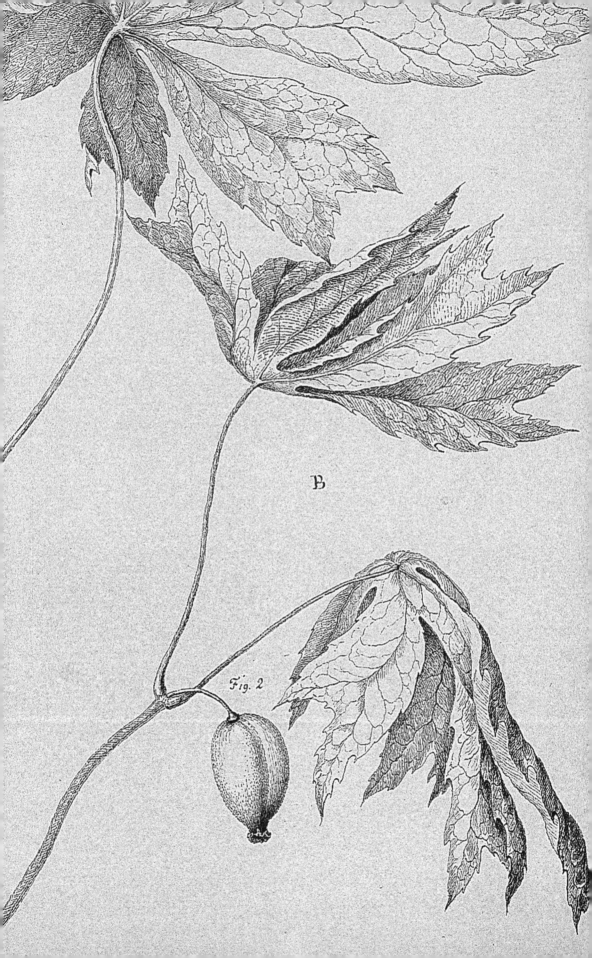

B

Fig. 2

MICHAEL GAUDIO

Surface and Depth

The Art of Early American Natural History

Natural history has always been a visual science. Sir Francis Bacon, at the beginning of the sixteenth century, articulated its visual foundations in his *Great Instauration* (1620), in which he called for a new objectivity that was to be grounded in ocular experience:

> And all depends on keeping the eye steadily fixed upon the facts
> of nature and so receiving their images simply as they are. For God
> forbid that we should give out a dream of our own imagination for
> a pattern of the world.[1]

For Bacon, the natural historian was to remain passive before nature as its images were received by the eye alone, free from any interfering thoughts. It was only through such disciplined looking that the observer could curb the human penchant for projecting one's own dreams and desires—God forbid—onto nature.

And yet, in spite of the enormous influence Bacon's views have exerted on the history of scientific thought, practice, and institutions, the discovery of nature never has been a process carried out with an innocent eye. Generation after generation of

DETAIL OF FIGURE 18 William Bartram, *Podophyllum peltatum (Mayapple)*, n.d. Ink. American Philosophical Society.

natural historians have given out dreams of their own imaginations for patterns of the world. In the words of the historian Richard White, "no new land, no new place is ever *terra incognita*. It always arrives to the eye fully stocked with expectations, fears, rumors, desires and meanings."[2] And it is precisely because of this fact that scholars of early American natural history imagery have become accustomed to treating "nature" itself as a historically conditioned category onto which artists such as Mark Catesby, William Bartram, Alexander Wilson, John James Audubon, and Titian Ramsey Peale each projected his own expectations, fears, and desires.[3]

Still, the art historian who is inclined to see more culture than nature in natural history illustration meets with some resistance before an image like the gouache of the bead snake (PLATE 8) by the British naturalist Mark Catesby (1682–1749), who later incorporated this figure into his *Natural History of Carolina, Florida, and the Bahama Islands* (1731–1743). What deep "desires and meanings," one might well ask, lie behind this apparently innocent view of nature's surfaces? Catesby, an artist firmly committed to the Baconian project of receiving the facts of nature "simply as they are," presents the viewer with a brilliantly colored snake seen in relation to nothing but the empty white ground across which it appears to slither. A slight shadow suggests that the creature rests on a plane parallel to and only centimeters below the picture plane, a format that makes the snake appear as if it were a specimen pinned to the page of a naturalist's album. By utterly decontextualizing his subject, Catesby defies the viewer to read the image as an individual's interpretation of nature. This is not nature seen by anyone in particular; it is simply nature *seen*.

To be sure, other works by Catesby invite more involved readings by giving the interpreter more to work with (SEE PLATE 9 and FIGURE 12). But even in its more complex compositions, as we shall see, natural history illustration is always at loggerheads with "depth," whether this depth is understood to be the projection of political ideology, psychological interiority, or simply theories about the organization of the natural world (a speculative activity that in the seventeenth and eighteenth centuries was more closely associated with the theorizing of the natural philosopher than with the fact-gathering of the natural historian).[4] A well-rounded picture of natural history illustration in colonial America and the early republic requires that we take its resistance to depth seriously. Certainly we should look for projections of the artist's "desires and meanings," but we also should remain aware of the artist's active resistance to such projections, his or her effort to stay at the level of the eye receiving nature's surfaces simply as they are. The aim of my essay is to demonstrate how the imagery of eighteenth- and early nineteenth-century artist–naturalists in the New World, especially

Mark Catesby and the Philadelphia naturalist William Bartram (1739–1823), may be understood as a dialogue *between* surface and depth, between transparent and accessible visual truths on the one hand, and more subjective, opaque, and for that reason more suspicious meanings—in the eyes of their contemporary audiences—on the other. "Dialogue" seems an appropriate term because surface and depth are interdependent: the natural historian's quest for a fully legible nature, one that is entirely surface, implies that there are obscure depths from which nature must be rescued or into which it could potentially sink. And in eighteenth-century America, there was some urgency in retrieving these visible surfaces, for natural history held the promise of discovering the universal knowledge that a broad public could agree upon, a set of indisputable truths that would not only provide a common foundation for further scientific work, but indeed for a whole project of nation building. As the Philadelphia physician Benjamin Rush noted, natural history was "the first study of the father of mankind, in the garden of Eden. It furnishes the raw materials of knowledge upon all subjects."[5] If the history of mankind itself had begun with an exercise in natural history, then why not the history of a new nation?

"Natural history," writes the historian and theorist Michel Foucault, "is nothing more than the nomination of the visible," a definition that makes it perfectly understandable why Rush would have chosen Adam's naming of the animals in Genesis as the originary episode of this science: "So out of the ground the Lord God formed every beast of the field and every bird of the air, and brought them to the man to see what he would call them; and whatever the man called every living creature, that was its name."[6] Foucault's definition, like the Genesis story, boils taxonomy down to its two irreducible elements: seeing and the naming of that which is seen. But what is the relationship between these two elements, and what bearing might that relationship have on natural history's dialogue between surface and depth? The task of the artist–naturalist, it would seem, is aligned with the former, with the God-like task of rendering nature's surfaces visible and ready for naming. Like Catesby with his bead snake, the artist–naturalist aspires to display nature's objects in their objective reality, independent of the individual mind that perceives them. But when it comes to naming (Adam's task), the artificial element of human language is introduced, and with language come all the ideas and patterns that the human mind inevitably projects onto the world. Bacon once again sounded the alarm by preaching against the dangers of words. When not held in check by the facts presented to the eye, Bacon warned, words could easily become "idols of the mind" that lead to faulty generalizations about nature.[7]

Such suspicions of language were manifested time and again in European and American natural history circles, and nowhere were those suspicions greater than in the circle of scientists, political thinkers, and artists surrounding Thomas Jefferson during the early years of the American republic. This group, whose patterns of thought the historian Daniel Boorstin sought to recover in *The Lost World of Thomas Jefferson* (1948), looked upon natural history as a foundational science. It taught Jefferson and colleagues like Benjamin Rush, botanist Benjamin Smith Barton, and artist–entrepreneur Charles Willson Peale to be suspicious of system, indeed of any pretensions toward theoretical generalization beyond the visible facts at hand. Whatever abstract order underlay nature was unintelligible; the seeker of knowledge must instead work with that which we are given by God—the specificity of nature's surfaces. Any abstractions, any movements from surface to depth, were recognized as accommodations (often necessary, to be sure) to our limited capacity for holding the entirety of nature's variety in our memory. "No two animals," writes Jefferson, are exactly alike; no two plants, nor even two leaves or blades of grass. . . . This infinitude of units or individuals being far beyond the capacity of our memory, we are obliged, in aid of that, to distribute them into masses, throwing into each of these all the individuals which have a certain degree of resemblance; to subdivide these again into smaller groups, according to certain points of dissimilitude observable in them, and so on until we have formed what we call a system of classes, orders, genera and species.[8]

Specifically, it was the system of species classification and binomial nomenclature of Swedish naturalist Carl Linnaeus that offered Jefferson and others the specific words for designating "classes, orders, genera and species." By the late eighteenth century, Linnaeus' taxonomical system based on the sexual characteristics of plants, originally set forth in his *Systema Naturae* of 1735, had become widely accepted in the New World. By providing a finite but seemingly comprehensive set of variables for the purposes of classification, Linnaeus taught the eighteenth-century American naturalist to transform the visible world into words and thus discover the underlying structure of nature.[9]

But however rigorous Linnaeus' system of naming was, however attentive to visual specifics, it was still an artificial system that could meet with resistance. William Bartram, for example, frustrated patrons like the London physician John Fothergill with his reluctance to take up a Linnaean format in his drawings of American plants. In 1774, while Bartram was on an extended sojourn through the southern colonies that eventually resulted in his *Travels through North and South Carolina, Georgia, East and West Florida* (1791), Fothergill's agent wrote to Bartram: "The Dr. mentions to me, Some of the Drawings you sent to him, to be nondescript: but would it not be better to Colour & describe them botanically [i.e., according to Linnaeus]."[10] Although it became customary over the course of the eighteenth century for botanical illustrators to "dissect" plants according to the Linnaean system, early in his career Bartram rarely followed this script. His *Hymenocallis caroliniana* (*Carolina Spiderlily*) (FIGURE 13), an ink drawing probably made on his southern travels, is typical of the drawings that Fothergill found both admirable for their draughtsmanship and frustrating in their refusal to systematize. The two flowers of this spider lily overlap as they become entwined in a kind of botanical embrace, a vibrant but confusing jumble of leaves, petals, and stamens. Bartram focuses so lovingly on the depiction of this particular specimen that, instead of showing a representative of a species, he produces a unique individual with its own personality (throughout his life Bartram invested plants with human qualities). But then, as a

FIGURE 13 William Bartram, *Carolina Spiderlily (Hymenocallis caroliniana)*, n.d. Brown ink. American Philosophical Society.

naturalist, Bartram's interests were less in showing how nature conforms to an underlying system than in presenting its surfaces as they appeared to the eye, whether those appearances corresponded to Linnaeus or not. As Bartram claimed in the report he wrote for Fothergill based on his Southern travels:

> I attempt only to exhibit to your Notice, the outward furniture
> of Nature, or the productions of the Surface of the earth; without,
> troubling you with any notions, of their particular causes or design
> by Providence, such attempts I leave for the amusement of Men
> of Letters & Superior genius.[11]

Bartram's reluctance to make his art conform to the theories of men of "superior genius" is not to be confused with a lack of interest in nature's hidden depths (indeed Bartram's art, to which we will return, displays a fascination with depth), but it is symptomatic of how he, like other observers of New World flora and fauna throughout the eighteenth century, looked upon the visual recording of nature's surfaces as a corrective to the verbal account of nature. Images brought the viewer back to earth from the abstract "notions" of philosophy, or quite simply they offered the visual particulars in a way that even the most down-to-earth verbal description could not equal. It was for this reason that authors of eighteenth-century natural histories included, when they could afford it, illustrations in their texts. In the preface to his *Natural History*, Catesby writes:

> Illuminating Natural History is so particularly Essential to the perfect
> understanding of it, that I may aver a clearer Idea may be conceiv'd
> from the Figures of Animals and Plants in their proper Colours, than
> from the most exact Description without them: Wherefore I have
> been less prolix in the Discription.[12]

While the verbal descriptions that accompany Catesby's plates are essential to his book, word remains subordinate to image. The core of Catesby's project is the collection of watercolor drawings that was a product of years of travel and observation in America. When he found that sending the drawings elsewhere to be engraved would be prohibitively expensive, he took up the study of etching himself. Ultimately Catesby created 220 images the role of which in the *Natural History* is to empty nature of words, to return the New World to a prelinguistic state of pure visibility. The goal was not to avoid the dangers of language entirely—as if that were possible—but to prepare the world anew for natural history's Adamic task of naming.

While Catesby thought of his "illuminations" as correctives to verbal description, they nevertheless represent their author's own distinctive vision of the natural world. For example, in his *Bison Americanus and Rose Acacia* (PLATE 9), which like many other plates in the *Natural History* plays loosely with scale, Catesby brings together two entirely different species, a plant and an animal, and even draws a visual analogy between the dangling Acacia branch and the bison's own dangling tail. Through such visual means, Catesby projects his own nascent awareness of environmental inter-dependence onto the New World by suggesting a special relation between the bison and a species of tree upon whose leaves, the author notes, this animal likes to browse.[13] Catesby, in fact, received some criticism for his willingness to project his own precon-ceptions about the natural order into his pictures. Alexander Garden, a prominent British physician and naturalist, complained that Catesby's "sole object was to make showy figures of the productions of nature, rather than to give correct and accurate representations. This is rather to invent than to describe; it is indulging the fancies of his own brain, instead of contemplating and observing the beautiful works of God."[14] Catesby's "showiness" is even more evident in his *White Curlew* (FIGURE 12), an etching that displays the bird (a white ibis) against the leaf and stalk of a Bahamian plant known as the Golden Club. The juxtaposition of plant and animal again calls our attention to visual rhymes between plant and animal—the projecting bud at the tip of the stalk echoed by the beak, the beak echoed by the curve of the leaf. Catesby thus suggests a relation between divergent forms, but in this instance the substance of that relation is ambiguous. While Catesby's bison seems to interact with the Acacia tree, we wonder what the curlew might do with the golden club? Would the bird eat it? Nest in it? The ties between this bird and plant are entirely visual, entirely surface.

Like any artist, Catesby manipulates his subject matter to make it conform to his own sense of design. But even in a composition like the *White Curlew*, the artist still insists that it is the surfaces we perceive, and not language or the thoughts of the individual perceiver, that constitute the true source of natural knowledge. Indeed, Catesby's privileging of surfaces is reflected quite literally in his preference for flat, two-dimensional representation over the illusion of three-dimensional depth. "As I was not bred a Painter," writes Catesby, "I hope some faults in Perspective, and other Niceties, may be more readily excused, for I humbly conceive Plants, and other Things done in a Flat, tho' exact manner, may serve the Purpose of Natural History, better in some Measure than in a more bold and Painter like Way."[15]

FIGURE 14   Georges Louis
Leclerc, comte de Buffon,
*Histoire naturelle, générale,
et particulière . . .* , 1766.
Engraved plate of *American
Bison*. University of California,
Berkeley.

For Catesby, innocence of traditional pictorial training turns out to be a positive
boon when it comes to natural history illustration, for it results in a more direct
presentation of nature free from the "niceties" of artistic training. Catesby's "Flat,
tho' exact manner" is his means of achieving complete legibility, for if there are no
pictorial depths in images like the *Bison Americanus* and the *White Curlew*, if all forms
are flattened against the picture plane like pressed flowers, then the viewer must
presume that nothing of importance is hidden from view.

The illustration of the American Bison from Buffon's monumental *Histoire
naturelle générale et particulière* (1749–1789) offers an instructive comparison to
Catesby's manner insofar as it exemplifies a "more bold and Painter like" approach to
the natural history subject (FIGURE 14). The engraving of the *Bison Jubatus* (the Maned
Bison) is typical of Buffon's plates in that the artist adheres to perspective (ground and
sky both lead the eye to an implied vanishing point at the horizon, below the bison's
beard) and to other "niceties" (rolling clouds, rocky crags, even a buffalo chip) to
provide the setting for this portrait. In rejecting such an illusionistic format for his own
bison, Catesby rejects a pictorial mode that is defined first and foremost by its *relation*

to the viewer. That is to say, a strict perspectival format constructs its illusionistic world as the spatial projection of a single, immobile eye.

Buffon's illustration, while its perspective may not be rigorous, nevertheless implies a human viewpoint from which nature is seen—a condition that is acknowledged by the bison himself as he stares back at us, thus implicating the viewer in the perception of the natural world. This manner of presentation is in keeping, moreover, with Buffon's own theories about the natural order. Buffon was dedicated to the idea that nature's laws can never be known "in themselves." Instead, he argued that we can learn them only by relating our perceptions of nature to that which we do know—ourselves. For Buffon, the natural order was of necessity a projection of our own human natures onto the world, and for this reason the first animals he discusses in his *Histoire naturelle* are those most familiar to humans: animals like the horse, the sheep, and the dog.[16]

If Catesby's aperspectival surface views of American flora and fauna run counter to Buffon's human-centered theory of natural order and the human-centered mode of representation found in his plates, then we might well ask why Catesby took the course

FIGURE 15 Charles Willson Peale, *The Exhumation of the Mastodon*, 1806–1808. The Maryland Historical Society, Baltimore, Maryland.

he did. One is inclined to explain the pronounced flatness of Catesby's *Natural History* plates as evidence of an untrained artist's naiveté, and indeed Catesby himself, as we have seen, makes the claim of ignorance. But perhaps it is also possible to understand Catesby's naiveté as an important and indeed highly considered strategy of Enlightenment knowledge-making. Free from a "true" artist's sophistication and unburdened by the speculative impulses of a Buffon, the naïve artist–naturalist sees, with child-like innocence, a world of pure and unadulterated form. Even if it may occasionally result in a certain awkwardness—the slightly Picassoid visage of Catesby's bison, for example—Catesby's is a studied simplicity the objective of which is a vision *without* perspective, one that divests nature of the peculiarities and overzealousness of individual human intellects. This naïve impulse, moreover, is one that would be embraced by and developed in the thought of Jefferson and his circle, for whom a strategic naiveté was necessary to save democratic society from the perils of systematic thought. Too many competing ideas were dangerous in a democracy, leading to dispute and faction. If, however, the facts could be viewed simply as they are, with innocent eyes, then Americans could enjoy a "democracy of facts."[17]

And natural history could show the way. Indeed, the phrase democracy of facts was coined by Benjamin Smith Barton in an essay published in 1796 that attempted to demystify the widely held belief that the rattlesnake had the power to hypnotize its victims: "Perhaps, facts are never related in all their unadultrated [*sic*] purity except by those, who intent upon the discovery of truth, keep system at a distance, regardless of its claims. The strong democracy of facts should exert its wholesome sway."[18] Throughout his career Barton attempted to live up to this innocent search for "unadultrated purity" by collecting natural history studies (many of which survive in Barton's papers at the American Philosophical Society) from a variety of artists. The architect and engineer Benjamin Henry Latrobe, for example, supplied Barton with several watercolors of rattlesnakes, including one remarkable image that displays, with a combination of elegance and painstaking detail, a rattlesnake skeleton (PLATE 10).[19] Extending in waves across a three-foot sheet with an almost hypnotizing regularity, the individual ribs and vertebrae of the rattler, one after another, insist upon their particularity, even as the individual meaning of each segment becomes apparent only through its relation to the entirety of the skeletal structure. The image is a *tour de force* of visual attention. It stands as visual argument for the primacy of the visible detail within an emerging democracy of facts.

The relations among vision, bone structure, and social structure are drawn more explicitly in one of the early republic's great pictorial statements about natural history, Charles Willson Peale's *Exhumation of the Mastodon*, completed in 1808 (FIGURE 15).

FIGURE 16 Titian Ramsay Peale, *Mastodon Skeleton (Mammut americanum)*, 1821. Ink and wash. American Philosophical Society.

The painting reconstructs the unearthing of the bones of the prehistoric creature in 1801 from a flooded marl pit in the marshes of Newburgh, New York, a process that involved the removal of water from the pit with a giant sluice designed by Peale himself. Peale recovered enough bones from the site to reconstruct a nearly complete mastodon skeleton—pictured in an 1821 watercolor by Titian Ramsay Peale (FIGURE 16)—which became the great attraction of the Peale museum in Philadelphia. In the museum, this literal reconstruction served as a powerful metaphor not only for Peale's curatorial goal of reconstructing the world in miniature, but also for a nation devoted to the "mammoth" task of self-construction, a task that in Peale's picture is being performed by the community of laborers, naturalists, mothers, fathers, and children who inhabit the scene.[20]

The painting, which hung next to the skeleton in the "Mammoth Room" of the museum, makes a strong case for the centrality of the visual image in this labor of knowledge-making and nation-building. While Peale made the significant choice of commemorating this historical event in a visual medium, he also foregrounds a natural history image within the busy scene itself. To the right of the pit, Peale and family members all stand behind a giant, partially unfurled scroll that, instead of bearing words, bears a visual message about the skeletal structure of the mastodon's leg. From his high vantage point, grasping the end of the scroll, Peale gestures down toward a worker at the center of the pit who has just unearthed a bone that appears to match one of those pictured on the enormous sheet. In this notable episode of early American natural history, the artist's image proves to be an indispensable guide in rescuing nature's truths from the obscure depths of the marl pit. Visual evidence, Peale's *Exhumation of the Mastodon* suggests, constitutes the "bones" of the nation by providing the incontestable surfaces upon which both science and polity can be structured.

Peale, Barton, Jefferson—all these naturalists of the early republic—shared an ease in making intellectual and artistic leaps between visibility in the natural order and visibility in the social order.[21] The same can be said for the work of William Bartram, who explored this theme in a body of visual and written work that is as accomplished as it is idiosyncratic. Bartram's 1796 ink drawing *Arethusa divaricata* (*Rosebud Orchid*) (PLATE 11) draws a parallel between the community of plants in the foreground and, in the distance, a human community (perhaps Philadelphia). At the center of the composition stands the rosebud orchid and to its left another species of orchid that, as Bartram notes below the image, "is a native of Pennsylvania and Nw. Jersey." Indeed all the plants in the foreground, including the Venus flytrap, are native to North America. All share, moreover, the same little hillock: Bartram, following Catesby's lead, represents nature as a world of environmental interaction in which diverse plants and creatures exist together harmoniously.[22] Despite their variety, this is a peaceable botanical kingdom in which the menacing Venus flytrap lies down with the gentle orchid. It provides a model for the community on the far shore where church steeples rise vertically into the sky as a distant reflection of the verticals of the orchids. Along the river, a lone figure paddles a canoe. Perhaps this is the naturalist himself as he makes his daily commute between nature and society.

Five years before he made this drawing, Bartram published his classic of eighteenth-century natural history writing. The *Travels* is an extraordinary book for many reasons, not least of all for its resistance to all categories we might impose upon it. It is at once literary and scientific. It develops a proto-Romantic view of the natural world that was influential on the poetry of Wordsworth and Coleridge, but at the same time it stands as a true work of Enlightenment natural history in its privileging of absolute visibility in nature.[23] Of particular interest here, in an essay on the art of natural history, is the status of vision in the *Travels*.[24] Bartram's book serves as a useful guide to the interpretation of his visual works, such as the *Arethusa Divaricata*, for in the *Travels* nature is fundamentally a social world in which the flora and fauna of the southeastern United

States play out a politics of visibility.

While traveling along the Little St. Johns River in northern Florida, for instance, Bartram looks down at the fish swimming beneath him and receives a lesson in good citizenship. When the author looks over toward the banks of the river, where the water is muddy and opaque, he sees fish fighting each other for survival,

> yet when those different tribes of fish are in the transparent channel,
> their very nature seems absolutely changed; for here is neither
> desire to destroy nor persecute, but all seems peace and friendship.
> Do they agree on a truce, a suspension of hostilities? or by some
> secret divine influence, is desire taken away? or are they otherwise
> rendered incapable of pursuing each other to destruction.[25]

Bartram's questions are rhetorical. He knows, as does his reader, that the fight for survival ceases in the transparent waters because the "different tribes" can no longer practice deceit when everything is public knowledge. Elsewhere in the *Travels*, Bartram answers his own questions when he describes a crystalline pool inhabited by a variety of aquatic creatures: "The water or element in which they live and move is so perfectly clear and transparent, it places them all on an equality with regard to their ability to injure or escape from one another."[26] While the murky banks of the Little St. Johns reverse this utopian condition, in the transparent channel there is no opportunity for secret plotting or stealthy ambushes. The dangers of opaque depths are mitigated when all is transparent surface.

The aquatic politics of the Little St. Johns share in a broader politics of visibility in the early years of the republic. During the late eighteenth century, America experienced a "rhetorical revolution," as the literary historian Jay Fliegelman has described it. This was a cultural revolution in which conventional modes of public expression were rejected and replaced with a new sincerity in self-presentation. Writers and orators now insisted on a "natural language"—one "composed not of words themselves, but of the tones, gestures, and expressive countenances with which a speaker delivered those words," a language that would guarantee a truthful revelation of character by transforming one's body into evidence of a sincere, interior self.[27] Depth, in other words, would become visible on the surface. This natural language, moreover, was a democratic language, a corollary to Barton's "democracy of facts." It would be essential for the creation of a society in which, in the words of the eighteenth-century historian David Ramsey, "mankind appear as they really are without any false coloring."[28]

Thus when Jefferson, in the Declaration of Independence, speaks of the "self-

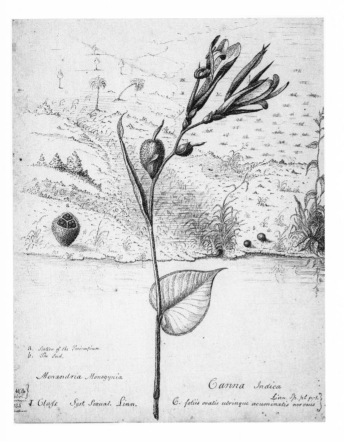

a. *Section of the Pericarpium*
b. *The Seed.*

Monandria Monogynia

1784
I *Class Syst Sexual. Linn.*

Canna Indica

Linn. Sp pl p:1.
C. *foliis ovatis utrinque acuminatis nervosis*

evident" truth that "all men are created equal," he makes a claim very similar to Bartram's verbal claim about the equality of fish in the transparent waters, or to Bartram's visual claim about the equality of plants on the riverbank: in all these cases, equality is premised upon the mutual visibility of subjects. For the politician as for the natural historian (Jefferson, of course, was both), the people, plants, and animals of the world could be fully and fairly represented when and only when one could read their essential natures transparently upon the surfaces they presented to the world.

The early republic's preoccupation with natural language and self-evidence allows us to see with more clarity the social and political imperatives that helped fuel the impulse toward "self-evidence" in Bartram's art and that of other artist–naturalists at work at the time. But Bartram, as much as he delights in the visibility of nature, also is unique for offering us something else: surfaces that cannot be allowed to stand on their own terms but are involved dialectically with nature's inscrutable depths. Perhaps the fullest expression of this dialectic is found in one of the great visual statements of eighteenth-century American natural history, Bartram's drawing in brown ink titled *The Great Alachua Savana in East Florida* (PLATE 12), created around 1775.

FIGURE 18 William Bartram, *Podophyllum peltatum (Mayapple)*, n.d. Ink. American Philosophical Society.

The viewer's eye enters the picture by roaming around the closely observed elements of the foreground, including a large palm tree on the left shaped like a stately Doric column (a detail that calls our attention to Bartram's Enlightenment respect for rational nature).[29] But quickly the eye plunges vertiginously into the distance and a landscape view of the savanna, its hydrography, and surrounding forests. Here the viewer's eye, occupying the same high vantage point enjoyed by the three cranes flying across the sheet on the right, is free to roam around vast distances, indeed to imagine the infinitude of nature itself. The landscape view occupies an ambiguous space in between a descriptive landscape and the symbolic format of a map. A handful of deer and cranes on the savanna, for instance, suggest a landscape teeming with these animals, a few regularly interspersed trees signify dense forests, and a single wooden structure stands for a whole Seminole village. One is reminded of Jefferson's statement about the limits of human memory before the infinite variety of nature, and the consequent need to call on man-made categories as accommodations to our limited memories. Bartram's symbolic elements and somewhat schematic view perform a similar function: they stand in for a vastness, a depth, in nature that cannot be described in the way the artist has precisely described the foreground elements. And yet this map-like landscape also is—as maps will be—quite flat. The leaf-like structure of the savanna adheres to the picture plane in the same fashion as the flattened leaf of the golden club in Catesby's *White Curlew*. The drawing cannot decide whether it is two dimensional or three dimensional, whether it wants to render the savanna legible by bringing it to the surface of the page, or imply nature's infinitude through the suggestion of measureless pictorial depths. This is a tension we find in many works by Bartram. In his 1784 drawing of the *Canna indica* (*Red Canna*) (FIGURE 17), for example, the flower bridges two distinct spheres: above, a landscape that extends into the distance, gradually fading from view; below, a space that is ostensibly a body of water bordering the landscape but which in fact serves as an empty, flat field coincident with the page itself and against which Bartram can effectively display the flat surface of the canna's leaf.

There is, finally, one more dimension to the play between surface and depth in Bartram's art, one that is evident even in a relatively straightforward botanical study like the *Podophyllum peltatum* (*Mayapple*) (FIGURE 18), in which we sense two different worlds in dialogue: the subterranean world of roots and the visible realm of the earth's surface. In Bartram's *The Great Alachua Savana*, this dialogue between above and below revolves around the sink hole located at the top center of the drawing. In the *Travels*, sink holes are sites that function as portals between "the productions of the Surface of the earth" (the manifest contents of natural history) and nature's invisible, mysterious depths. For Bartram, these sink holes operate according to a double logic: they are the great "mouths" of nature that swallow up the world of visible surfaces and they also are the sources, he calls them "fountains," from which the visibility of nature emerges. The sink hole in Bartram's view of the Alachua savanna, referred to as the "Great Sink" in the *Travels*, may be read visually as an abyss into which the waters of the landscape drain; but it could equally be interpreted as the very source of those waters. The dark, circular sink, certainly the most distinctive feature on this landscape, appears as a site of condensed energies that seems to nourish the savanna through streams that resemble the life-giving veins of a leaf. Bartram even refers to the Great Sink in the *Travels* as a "fatal fountain or receptacle," but he does not tell us which one it is.[30] It is both: it is a void *from* which the visibility of nature proceeds and *into* which it must return.

One of Bartram's distinctive contributions to the art of early American natural history is this effort to figure the limits of natural history's project of rendering the surfaces of the world visible, a project that in the 1770s informed a whole American culture of visibility. While Thomas Jefferson acknowledged that "the plan of creation is inscrutable to our limited faculties," Bartram actually found a place for that inscrutability by taking the dialogue between nature's surfaces and depths as the very subject of his art.[31] And in hinting at those depths, Bartram created within his natural history imagery a space that invites us to do that which Bacon feared most—a space in which we might "give out dreams of our own imagination for a pattern of the world."[32]

Endnotes

1. Francis Bacon, *A Selection of His Works*, ed. Sidney Warhaft (New York: The Odyssey Press, 1965), 323.

2. Richard White, "Discovering Nature in North America," *Journal of American History* 79 (December 1992): 874.

3. Two recent collections of essays that offer insightful readings of the visual culture of natural history in eighteenth- and early nineteenth-century America are Amy R.W. Meyers and Margaret Beck Pritchard, eds., *Empire's Nature: Mark Catesby's New World Vision* (Chapel Hill: University of North Carolina Press, 1998), and Amy R.W. Meyers, ed., *Art and Science in America: Issues of Representation* (San Marino: Huntington Library, 1998).

4. A good example of the kind of purely quantitative observations that the traveler/naturalist was expected to make in determining the natural history of North America or any other territory may be found in Robert Boyle's *General Heads for the Natural History of a Country* (London, 1692).

5. Quoted in Daniel J. Boorstin, *The Lost World of Thomas Jefferson* (Boston: Beacon Press, 1948), 272.

6. Michel Foucault, *The Order of Things: An Archaeology of the Human Sciences* (New York: Vintage Books, 1970), 132; Genesis 3:19, *The New Oxford Annotated Bible*, ed. Herbert G. May and Bruce M. Metzger (New York: Oxford University Press, 1973), 4.

7. This is a theme found throughout Bacon's writings. In a discussion of the syllogism, for instance, Bacon writes that the syllogism "consists of propositions, propositions of words, and words are the tokens and signs of notions. Now if the very notions of the mind (which are as the soul of words and the basis of the whole structure) be improperly and over-hastily abstracted from facts, vague, not sufficiently definite, faulty, in short, in many ways, the whole edifice tumbles." Bacon, *A Selection*, 314.

8. Quoted in Boorstin, 137.

9. On Linnaeus' transcription of visibility into discourse, see Foucault, 125–165.

10. Lyonel Chalmers to William Bartram, May 17, 1774, American Philosophical Society, typescript of original in Historical Society of Pennsylvania.

11. William Bartram, "Travels in Georgia and Florida 1773–74: A Report to Dr. John Fothergill," in Bartram, *Travels and Other Writings*, ed. Thomas P. Slaughter (New York: Library of America, 1996), 440.

12. Catesby, *The Natural History of Carolina, Florida and the Bahama Islands*, vol. 1 (London, 1754), xi–xii.

13. On Catesby and environmental thought, see Amy R. Weinstein Meyers, "Sketches from the Wilderness: Changing Conceptions of Nature in American Natural History Illustration: 1680–1880" (Ph.D. dissertation, Yale University, 1985), 46–112; and Meyers, "Picturing a World in Flux: Mark Catesby's Response to Environmental Interchange and Colonial Expansion," in *Empire's Nature*, 228–261.

14. Quoted in Victoria Dickenson, *Drawn From Life: Science and Art in the Portrayal of the New World* (Toronto: University of Toronto Press, 1998), 149.

15. Catesby, xi.

16. On the place of Buffon's *Histoire naturelle* within the history of animal illustration, see Alex Potts, "Natural Order and the Call of the Wild: the Politics of Animal Picturing," *Oxford Art Journal* 13, (1) (1990): 12–33.

17. On Jefferson's suspicions of ideas and system and his cultivation of naiveté, see Boorstin, 128–139.

18. Benjamin Smith Barton, *A Memoir Concerning the Fascinating Faculty which has been ascribed to the Rattlesnake, and other American Serpents* (Philadelphia, 1796), 35.

19. I am indebted to Alexander Nemerov for the identification of Latrobe as the maker of this watercolor.

20. For an illuminating interpretation of Peale's painting in the context of labor and politics in the early republic, see the chapter entitled "Peale's Mammoth" in Laura Rigal, *The American Manufactory: Art, Labor, and the World of Things in the Early Republic* (Princeton: Princeton University Press, 1998).

21. As Christopher Looby writes, "In the thought of cultural leaders of the early national period, there is a kind of automatic metaphorical exchange between images of natural order and ideas of social and political order." See Looby, "The Constitution of Nature: Taxonomy as Politics in Jefferson, Peale, and Bartram," *Early American Literature* 22 (1987): 252–273.

22. On Bartram and environmental thought, see Meyers, "Sketches from the Wilderness," 152–193.

23. On the privileging of vision in Bartram's *Travels*, see esp. Wayne Franklin, *Discoverers, Explorers, Settlers: The Diligent Writers of Early America* (Chicago: University of Chicago Press, 1979), 67; and Christoph Irmscher, *The Poetics of Natural History: From John Bartram to William James* (New Brunswick: Rutgers University Press, 1999), 33–55.

24. For a fuller development of some of the following remarks on Bartram, vision, and natural history illustration, see Michael Gaudio, "Swallowing the Evidence: William Bartram and the Limits of Enlightenment," *Winterthur Portfolio* 36, (1) (2001): 1–17.

25. Bartram, *Travels*, 197–198. On the politics of strife in Bartram's *Travels*, see Douglas Anderson, "Bartram's *Travels* and the Politics of Nature," *Early American Literature* 25 (1990): 3–17.

26. Bartram, *Travels*, 150.

27. Jay Fliegelman, *Declaring Independence: Jefferson, Natural Language, and the Culture of Performance* (Stanford: Stanford University Press, 1993), 2.

28. Quoted in Fliegelman, 33.

29. For an exceptional close reading of this drawing, see Meyers, "Sketches from the Wilderness," 131–145.

30. Bartram, *Travels*, 150–151.

31. Thomas Jefferson, *Writings*, ed. Merrill D. Peterson (New York: The Library of America, 1984), 1330.

32. It is in the mysterious depths evoked in Bartram's *Travels* that Coleridge projected his own dream of *Kubla Kahn*. Inspired by Bartram's description of the play between surface and depth through the fountains and sink holes of Florida, Coleridge writes of the sacred, subterranean river Alph that is interrupted in its "deep romantic chasm" when "a mighty fountain . . . flung up momently the sacred river." On Bartram's influence on Coleridge's *Kubla Khan*, see John Livingston Lowes, *The Road to Xanadu: A Study in the Ways of the Imagination* (Boston: Houghton Mifflin, 1927), 332–340.

half Natural Size.

A. Male flower
B Female Do.
C. A single
   flower 20 t
   natural Si
D A single
   flower
E. A flower
   Galopin

A

D

C

Streblanthus auriculatus

C. S. Rafinesque

JOYCE E. CHAPLIN

Nature and Nation

Natural History in Context

Is there a specifically *American* natural history? This question highlights a key feature of the natural sciences from the eighteenth into the nineteenth centuries: a tension between the universal and the national. If naturalists increasingly insisted that they defined information about nature that was meaningful in all parts of the globe, their efforts nevertheless were conditioned by their national loyalties and by their generic identity as Europeans, or, in the colonies, as inheritors of and participants in European culture. Nature may, in theory, have possessed properties valid in all places, but knowledge of these properties seemed grounded in particular national cultures. The tension between universality and nationality is nowhere more apparent than in the British colonies that would revolt against empire and establish an independent republic, the United States of America.

The American Revolution itself was a paradoxical blend of the national and the universal, an Enlightenment-era marriage of chauvinism and cosmopolitanism. Although they had once been devoted to British nationalism and empire, the American patriots argued that they—not the British—defended the universal "rights of man." But the patriots made this claim even as they championed particular American liberties

OPPOSITE, DETAIL OF FIGURE 20 C. S. (Constantine Samuel) Rafinesque, *"Streblanthus auriculatus . . . half Natural Size,"* n.d. Graphite and ink. American Philosophical Society.

and embraced, for the first time, a distinctive American identity constructed on a simplified society and economy and on proximity to Native Americans and to wilderness. To examine nature in the United States was to advertise the nation's wonders and its citizens' intellectual prowess, even as that examination had to work hard to mask the overwhelming cultural backwardness of the early republic. That natural history in America was inflected by nationality was therefore both intentional (promoting the American-ness of certain phenomena and practices) and unintentional, as when socioeconomic realities dictated which practices had precedence.

Although Americans' most interesting contributions were made to natural history, that was only part of the field of contemporary natural science. *Natural philosophy* was the more theoretical portion of the sciences; it included such abstract fields as mathematics and physics as well as conjectures about the construction of matter and the basis of living material. *Natural history* encompassed more concrete and descriptive fields—such as the study of plants and animals—that we would call the *life sciences*. But it also investigated climate, geography, human life, and even human cultures, matters now labeled the *social sciences*. If natural philosophy defined abstract or universal questions, natural history was very often connected to regional or national interests. (But natural philosophy and natural history were not perfectly separate enterprises, and developments in one often affected the other.) Before American independence, colonial naturalists made their most distinctive contributions to a natural history that underwrote British power and deferred to European-defined theories of nature; after the American Revolution, United States naturalists struggled to overcome this colonial framework, but they failed to establish themselves in fields outside natural history, instead relying on its descriptive methods of study to argue for their nation's distinctiveness.

American naturalists thus always vied with their British (and European) counterparts and used natural history to support their national status first as British–Americans, then as citizens of the United States. In Britain, the natural sciences would acquire new authority to redefine imperial goals; in the United States, the sciences would lose institutional autonomy and confidence. Most American naturalists failed to make intellectual contributions that would have silenced Old World critics of the new republic's backwardness. Americans therefore used natural history to emphasize the particular features of their material circumstances, clearly aligning nature and nation. Yet many Europeans continued to think of American naturalists as non-theorizers who merely documented flora and fauna. Interestingly, the post-1776 American naturalist who had the greatest impact abroad was William Bartram. Bartram's emphasis on nature's ineffable qualities was strikingly different from the focus in Britain (and western Europe generally) on science as an instrument of authority over nature. This difference was an indication of the distinctive national character that natural history had acquired in the United States as citizens of the republic sought to redefine their relation to the natural world and to Old World culture.

By the early eighteenth century, the "new science" associated especially with Isaac Newton set important standards for defining properties of nature that were observable to humans, manipulable in experiments, capable of being expressed in mathematics, and, above all, universally applicable. These criteria (especially the experimental and mathematical qualities) were, however, most easily achieved in "mechanics" (physics), as in Newton's own studies. Some individuals endeavored to apply Newtonian science to "the animate creation," as Stephen Hales did for respiration and circulation in plants and animals in the 1720s and 1730s. Although Newtonian science was the clearest statement of belief that the natural world had universal laws, over the course of the eighteenth century, this approach declined somewhat in influence, particularly after Newton's death in 1727.[1]

Newtonianism had limited impact also because it was popularly understood as a species of materialism, a belief in a cold, mechanical world devoid of any divine spark. (Nothing could have been further from Newton's own views.) The extreme materialist position, which postulated that the universe and its inhabitants (including humans) were soul-less machines, had some adherents but many more vociferous critics. Religious critics of materialism, who suspected it as deism or even atheism, were powerful in this regard. Some religious radicals stressed a continuous, divine presence in the physical world and ascribed mystical powers to matter. Established figures in the European sciences sought a middle way, examining matter's physical properties without denying a divine Creator or human souls; the Royal Society, Britain's premier learned body and oldest scientific institution, tried especially to keep mysticism at bay.[2]

Naturalists also pursued an older strategy to make sense of the natural world: classification. Schemes to put all creatures into discrete categories had existed since the ancient Greeks. Classification systems proliferated during the Renaissance, as Europeans struggled to order the ever-increasing specimens and reports that streamed in from extra-European territories. By the eighteenth century, the Swedish botanist Carl von Linné (Carolus Linnaeus) defined binomial classes that emphasized, for plants and animals, each species' mode of sexual reproduction; Linnaeus' schema, which, with modifications, survives until the present day, was the first system that aspired to a universal theory of categorization. New York colonist Cadwallader

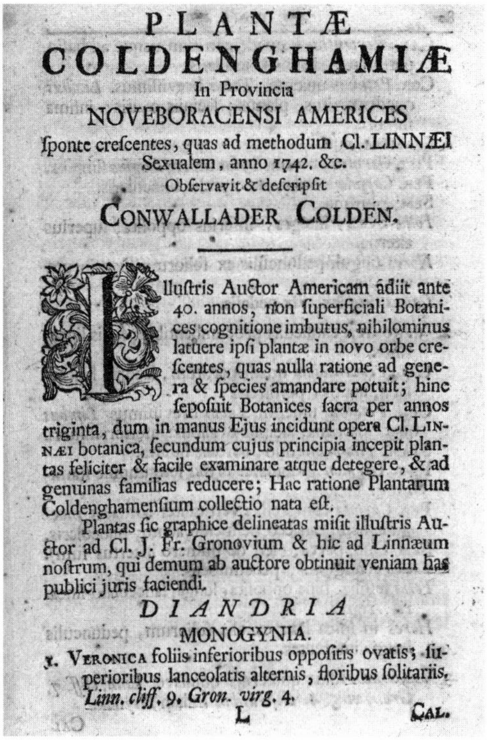

PLANTÆ
COLDENGHAMIÆ
In Provincia
NOVEBORACENSI AMERICES
Sponte crescentes, quas ad methodum Cl. LINNÆI
Sexualem, anno 1742. &c.
Observavit & descripsit
CONWALLADER COLDEN.

Illustris Auctor Americam adiit ante
40. annos, non superficiali Botanices cognitione imbutus, nihilominus
latuere ipsi plantæ in novo orbe crescentes, quas nulla ratione ad genera & species amandare potuit; hinc
seposuit Botanices sacra per annos
triginta, dum in manus Ejus incidunt opera Cl. LIN-
NÆI botanica, secundum cujus principia incepit plan-
tas feliciter & facile examinare atque detegere, & ad
genuinas familias reducere; Hac ratione Plantarum
Coldenghamensium collectio nata est.
    Plantas sic graphice delineatas misit illustris Au-
ctor ad Cl. J. Fr. Gronovium & hic ad Linnæum
nostrum, qui demum ab auctore obtinuit veniam has
publici juris faciendi.

DIANDRIA
MONOGYNIA.
1. VERONICA foliis inferioribus oppositis ovatis; su-
perioribus lanceolatis alternis, floribus solitariis.
Linn. cliff. 9. Gron. virg. 4.
L   CAL.

FIGURE 19 Cadwallader Colden, *Plantae Coldenghamiae in Provincia Noveboracensi Americes sponte crescentes, quas ad methodum Cl. Linnaei Sexualem, anno 1742 &c.* Uppsala, 1749. American Philosophical Society.

Colden followed Linnaeus when he published his *Plantae Coldenghamiae in provincia Noveboracensi Americes sponte crescentes* (1749) (FIGURE 19). Linnaeus nevertheless had plenty of critics; older or rival systems of classification remained in use into the nineteenth century. In France, Antoine-Laurent de Jussieu formulated categories based on the characters of plant and animal embryos; United States resident José Francesco Correia da Serra favored Jussieu in his *Reduction of all the Genera of Plants contained in the Catalogus Plantarum Americae Septentrionalis, of the late Dr. Muhlenberg, to the Natural Families of Mr. de Jussieu's System* (1815).[3]

While much eighteenth-century natural history was written by and for experts, this was also a time when the natural sciences were popularized on an unprecedented scale. Audiences for lectures and demonstrations of natural phenomena were large and surprisingly engaged, relishing new experiences such as contact with electricity. Men and women alike shared the new interest in natural history, a topic that was present even in children's literature. The Linnaean system encouraged amateurs to "go botanizing," taking part in a transnational effort to vindicate a new system of knowledge. Periodicals, pamphlets, and books further explained these new discoveries. The best example of this printed popularization appeared in Oliver Goldsmith's

History of the Earth, and Animated Nature (1774), a widely disseminated text that presented natural history for a literate but unspecialized audience.[4]

As popular and learned interest in the natural sciences spread, British colonists were for the most part consumers rather than producers of new knowledge. The American who most successfully emulated the Newtonian project was Benjamin Franklin, whose experiments with electricity defined new physical properties and set a standard for elegance in experimental design and reportage. No other colonist came close to Franklin's prowess, however, and even Franklin failed to contribute to the mathematical component of Newton's work. Most colonists undertook non-Newtonian investigations, focusing on the descriptive essence of natural history, and they usually did so by providing Old World naturalists with specimens, texts, or images that these experts then interpreted. The intellectual connection between Europe and America therefore resembled its economic and political connections, with Americans largely subordinate to Europeans and mostly occupied in providing raw material to be refined in the metropolis.[5]

Colonists used natural history to flatter British patrons. Many American plants and animals received Latinized versions of the names of the great and the good. For instance, Mark Catesby named one flowering plant after Dr. Richard Mead, physician to the king and fellow of the Royal Society; an engraving in Catesby's *Natural History of Carolina, Florida, and the Bahama Islands* (1729–1747) shows the plant *Meadia* as a backdrop to one of his striking and characteristic bird illustrations (PLATE 13). Eager to see such creatures for themselves, British naturalists, patrons, and dealers specified how plants, animals, and minerals should be preserved for transatlantic shipment, as in John Ellis' *Directions for Bringing Over Seeds and Plants, from the East Indies and Other Distant Countries* (1770) (SEE FIGURE 9 ON PAGE 44).[6]

If circulation of specimens replicated colonial relations between Britain and America, the promotion of natural history likewise reinforced imperial goals. This was particularly the case with botany, which fostered commercial agriculture in the colonies and supplied exotics for the gardens of the British aristocracy and gentry. These activities, which supported chattel slavery in the colonies and social hierarchy in Britain, respectively, demonstrate how colonial naturalists operated within intellectual connections shaped by imperial politics. After the American Revolution, these were precisely the features that faded in the United States but flourished in Great Britain.[7]

The British connection between science and empire, in which the state sought to promote imperial aims, grew stronger despite (and perhaps because of) the American Revolution. In this regard, the British emulated the French, whose exploration and colonizing earlier in the eighteenth century had been strongly supported by royal authority and institutions. Large-scale expeditions, such as those of Captain James Cook into the Pacific during the 1760s and 1770s, are key examples of the British state modeling its efforts on those of the stronger and more absolutist French state. So too were colonial experimental gardens, each linked to the Royal Botanic Gardens at Kew, the showcase and warehouse of plants from an expanding British dominion. These activities were essential for the ruling elite's sense of purpose, especially in an era when imperialism and inherited forms of political authority were coming under attack. Sir Joseph Banks—aristocrat, explorer, naturalist, agricultural improver, and president of the Royal Society—was the essential figure in the realignment of science and empire. Banks promoted Kew Gardens as a center of botanical activities, deplored the rebellious American colonists, and encouraged new efforts at colonization that would remain firmly under British control.[8] Popular images of Banks both acknowledged and poked fun at his flamboyant role in British natural history and empire (PLATE 5).

Imperial control was sharply challenged during the age of the American and French revolutions. Two such challenges came from the lower classes and from religious dissenters. Many social groups in Britain were interested in the sciences, attending demonstrations and lectures, working for naturalists, and reading the proliferating popular texts on nature. But the Royal Society especially struggled to prevent unorthodox activities and interpretations from eroding a unified natural philosophy. That the privileged elements of British society, including aristocrats and Church of England clergy, managed to prevent political radicals and religious dissenters from influencing the dominant scientific discourse is remarkable. This dominance was fading on the margins, nevertheless. Scottish universities and the newer scientific academies of the provinces, for instance, accepted religious dissenters and were less tied to aristocratic or royal patronage.[9]

Religious controversy especially intersected with natural philosophy. The concept of animate nature raised significant questions about the basis of life and the status of humanity within a fundamentally material world. How had anything achieved existence and why did it continue to operate according to an ordered plan? Were humans, like plants and animals, mere machines? If they had souls, were these souls composed of matter? These had long been theological questions; new answers to them that stressed material processes were quite contentious. The fundamentals of life—generation, growth, regeneration, and degeneration—seemed difficult to describe in convincing and untroubling ways. Concepts of animate creation therefore retained or revived older ideas to describe living creatures and life forces. Ideas about spontaneous generation, for instance, enjoyed a long career, and attempts to avoid these ideas erred on the side of unhelpful vagueness.[10]

Erasmus Darwin, grandfather of the better-known Charles Darwin and one of the most influential British naturalists of the late eighteenth century, inspired responses ranging from confidence over the natural sciences to doubt that they explained anything about the physical world. Darwin was a physician, poet, and natural philosopher who examined many aspects of nature. (He also belonged to the influential Lunar Society, a circle in Birmingham that included the potter Josiah Wedgwood, steam-engine innovators Matthew Boulton and James Watt, and chemical experimenter Joseph Priestley.) While Darwin passionately maintained that the Christian God was the Creator, he also presented matter as self-organizing, as if removed from divine power. In his widely read *Zoonomia; or, The Laws of Organic Life* (1794–1796), Darwin argued that all warm-blooded animals descended from "one living filament" or pre-embryonic seminal vessel; the innate "laws of animation" regulated the generation and organization of organic particles into a natural world that humans could examine and understand.[11]

This proto-evolutionary interpretation unnerved many. Darwin presented animal (including human) life blindly moving forward through godless millennia, as if no higher power had ever touched the "one living filament." Further, insistence that these processes were rationally understandable intimated that humans eventually could imitate the divine creation, making new life as they saw fit. Striking religious critics as too materialist (why should matter be so self-orderly?) and scientific critics as too mystical (why was material order so underdefined?), Darwin's theories raised questions that would bedevil naturalists on both sides of the Atlantic.

In the meantime, the less theoretical portions of natural history, especially its descriptive and practical elements, would continue to promote Britain's imperial activities. Much recent work on the sciences that supported empire has emphasized the pacific nature of this enterprise. The "swing to the east" that characterized the formation of the second British empire (especially the Asian territories accumulated after the American Revolution) was marked supposedly by benevolent motives and non-military tactics. In essence, the British focused on trade more than on settlement, hoping to avoid the emergence of colonial interests that had precipitated revolt in North America and the conflict between natives and settlers that had worried British officials at least since the Seven Years War. Criticism of the Atlantic slave trade and the ultimate decision to abolish it likewise supported a sense that British imperialism and commerce had been softened and rendered more humane.[12]

That British science peacefully engaged non-European populations was particularly apparent in attempts to elicit knowledge about the natural world from peoples in Asia and Africa, including information for mapping and about botany. And while British (and European) men of science contributed to theories of race, separating Europeans from non-Europeans to argue the natural authority of the former, a competing tendency emphasized cultural similarities, especially in relation to Asian populations that Europeans regarded as "civilized"—possessed of written language and admirable technology. This trend appeared most notably in Sir William Jones' remarkable essay, *Asiatic Researches* (1786), that compared Sanskrit to the languages of Europe. Jones thereby established the field of historical philology that, for the moment, was significantly different from racialized contrasts that argued for physical differences among humans.[13]

This is not to say that the British saw non-Europeans as equals; for the most part, the sciences extolled the unique strengths of European cultures, and British naturalists eagerly inscribed their nation on the physical creation. In his *The Loves of the Plants* (1789), a poetic treatment of the Linnaean botanical system, which emphasized the sexual reproduction of plants, Erasmus Darwin presented a courtship both flowery and florid:

> MEADIA's soft chains *five* suppliant beaux confess,
> And hand in hand the laughing belle address;
> Alike to all, she bows with wanton air,
> Rolls her dark eye, and waves her golden hair.[14]

The plant that Mark Catesby had named for Dr. Richard Mead thus illustrated the sexualized view Linnaeus had laid over the natural world and advertised British prowess at naming all parts of that world.[15]

After the American Revolution, Americans followed developments in the British sciences, which they hoped to imitate. They failed, however, except in natural history. The British used science to connect and to advertise connections among the different parts of the world they sought to control. Americans, in contrast, used science to demonstrate their control over the natural world they had extracted from the British Empire, but this territory was not part of a global extension of dominion; it was continental and looked inward. The republic's learned societies and periodicals focused on regional problems and phenomena and had overwhelmingly state-based membership and readership. (The first national science periodical, Benjamin Silliman's *American Journal of Science and Arts*, would not emerge until 1818.) Although the American

Philosophical Society in Philadelphia has been held up as a counterpart to European learned societies, and despite attempts to present the Meriwether Lewis and William Clark expedition as the equivalent of French or British voyages of exploration, the United States could not yet rival such European accomplishments.[16]

These developments may seem paradoxical. The post-revolutionary period was one of amazing ferment in American politics and political thought. Why did this ferment not bubble over into every area? The exciting and new political foundations of the early republic were in fact what guaranteed the slow development of the sciences. This was true for two reasons: the lack of wealthy and prestigious patrons for scientific enterprises, and the federal nature of American politics and society.

The American Revolution severed connections to Britain's aristocracy and royal family, two significant sources of patronage. It was difficult even for aristocrats who were friends of American naturalists to extend courtesy, let alone funds. Sir Joseph Banks maintained his friendship with Benjamin Franklin, but dismissed other American naturalists. And within the United States, no privileged and wealthy class existed to support science. As Peter S. Du Ponceau (French-born scholar of native American languages) put it, "the Law, Physic [medicine], politics &c takes up the attention of most of our learned men. Every man here lives by his labour . . . & there are not enough of rich men to encourage scientific investigations."[17] Furthermore, the individual states could not possibly raise revenue for major scientific activities; the federal government would not. In 1801, astronomer Andrew Ellicott complained that "in this country I have not a single Astronomical correspondent, neither is it a science which has ever been patronised by either of the States, or by the general government."[18] The Lewis and Clark corps of discovery was (like the Louisiana purchase itself) the exception that proved the rule—the United States did not otherwise invest federal money in ambitious projects.[19]

Americans were not completely cut off from centers of scientific inquiry. United States allies, especially the French, gave pointed support to men of learning in the republic. American naturalists would continue to correspond with learned figures in Europe, they would publish papers in journals such as the *Philosophical Transactions* of the Royal Society, and they would identify new phenomena that they communicated across the Atlantic. But these were scattered achievements. Whatever contributions to science Americans made, there was a long period of take-off before they sustained a level of accomplishment comparable to that of Europeans; that moment arrived in the 1840s and 1850s, when American universities, scientific organizations, and journals would be comparable to their European counterparts and not require further apology.

Most of the sciences were, therefore, deferred opportunities for Americans to demonstrate their intellectual prowess in the face of European criticism. In the Euro-American world, scientific work, if it investigated universal properties, was the *dernier cri* in cultural development. By the late eighteenth century, chemistry, mathematics, and physics were the most difficult areas of the sciences, and thus had the greatest prestige. But these were precisely the areas in which American learning lagged until the second third of the nineteenth century. The deficiencies of the American natural sciences are highlighted by the few examples of what greater investment accomplished. It was not accidental that Harvard and West Point led the way in teaching modern mathematics, especially the new French texts that were redefining the field. That is, only two atypical centers, one of private wealth and the other of the federal government's bounty, absorbed innovations common in the European sciences.[20]

Citizens of the United States focused more on the nationally distinctive features of their natural world, and less on the sciences that leaned toward universal principles. Identifying America's natural phenomena was an important task, especially when it restated the United States' claims over its territories. Constantine S. Rafinesque, for example, brought the flora and fauna of Kentucky and Tennessee to national and international attention, as in his description and drawing of the flowering Streblanthus, "a New American Genus of Plants" (FIGURE 20). New botanical specimens received American names; German botanist Frederick Pursh created two genera, *Lewisia* and *Clarkia,* in his *Flora Americae Septentrionalis* (1814) and named no fewer than three species after Lewis. Still, patriotic critics of Pursh grumbled that his work was published in London, rather than in the United States, and that it used the generic "America" rather than the specific "United States" to designate the nativity of the new flora (PLATE 14).[21]

Furthermore, natural history was a tricky vehicle for nationalist pride because it exposed weaknesses in the United States' pretensions to learning. Scholars from both the Old and New Worlds maintained an interest in natural history's relevant subfields. The former were intrigued by American exotica, whereas the latter sought to make the most of whatever might be close to hand yet curious to Old World readers. But Americans resented European competitors, who nosily looked into matters that should provide foundations for national display of learning. An infusion of emigre naturalists was valuable, but raised the question of whether native practitioners would ever compete with those bred in Europe. And private finance rather than public funds supported most of the republic's ventures into natural history, as with Charles Willson Peale's museum in Philadelphia. Peale's exhibitions showed fine art and natural specimens

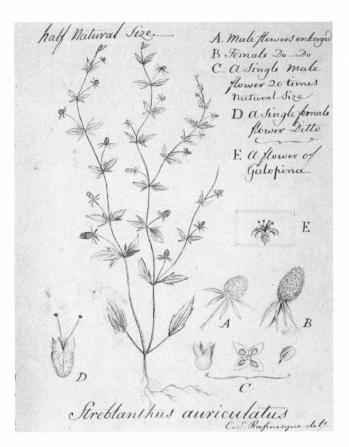

FIGURE 20

C. S. (Constantine Samuel)
Rafinesque, "Streblanthus
auriculatus . . . half Natural
Size," n.d. Graphite and
ink. American Philosophical
Society.

together, to impress on Americans (and foreign visitors) the accomplishments of republican citizens and the wonders of the natural world (PLATE 1).[22]

Alexander Wilson's career also revealed the strained connection between natural history and American nationalism. Wilson was one of the most talented naturalists of the early republic, offering a monumental, nine-volume *American Ornithology* (1808–1814) that illustrated and described all the known birds of North America. Wilson utilized specimens and information from his travels along the eastern seaboard and into the southwest, as well as from the Lewis and Clark expedition. His work was an important statement about the United States' newly continental ambition. Yet Wilson was a Scot and had been as devoted to Scottish nationalism as he would be to American nationalism; he was good evidence that the new republic welcomed intellectual merit, but not that the country could nurture its own geniuses. Nor did the *American Ornithology's* publication history vindicate a truly continental nationalism so much as it showed federalism's experimental nature, based on a provisional confederacy among individual states. Wilson's opus was published in one place, Philadelphia,

FIGURE 21 Thomas Jefferson, *Comparative Vocabulary of Native American Languages: Leaf with List of Languages and Names for Turtledove (?), Pheasant, and Partridge*, 1802–1808. American Philosophical Society.

with private subscriptions from individuals and institutions in different states. The federal government gave no direct support, and Wilson got many of his subscriptions because he himself tramped through the different states seeking patrons and scouting birds (PLATE 15). A continental and federal United States was, for the moment, little more than a promise of future greatness.[23]

Lack of greatness also threatened the United States because of its distance from European metropolitan centers and because its polity allegedly lacked the grounding in antiquity other nations enjoyed. Removal from the corruptions of the Old World and a stated goal to start the world "anew" were exciting opportunities for Americans in the early republic, but they carried a heavy price. What could natural history do to remedy the situation?

America's native populations provided one possible basis for the nation's antiquity. Several leaders in the early republic undertook ethnographic examination of American

Indians and excavation of ancient sites, such as those constructed by the "mound-builders" in the Ohio and Mississippi valleys. Thomas Jefferson, for example, argued for the valor of native peoples as a way to buttress white Americans' national pride. Like many others, Jefferson analyzed Indian languages, participating in a Euro-American craze to taxonomize all languages in order to determine their origins and interconnections (FIGURE 21). But white Americans were reluctant to praise Native Americans too much, lest this contradict claims of cultural superiority to and political authority over native peoples. This was a dilemma: to deny that Native Americans had an important and ancient cultural base was to lose one potential foundation for American society's equality with those of Europe and Asia; but to admit this ancient cultural base was to challenge the republic's racial order.[24]

This dilemma was apparent in the surprising admiration that Americans had for British India. From the Revolution through the first decade of the nineteenth century, India fascinated Americans, perhaps because they, as ex-colonists of the British empire, had just renounced access to it. Wonder at south Asian peoples, languages, flora and fauna was mixed with an identification with India's fate as a place that had entered the empire (in the 1760s) just before America left. The British "swing to the east" colored Americans' perceptions, leading them to see India as a place of fabulous wealth and vast populations of exotic yet civilized peoples. Although he had never met anyone from the subcontinent, Yale graduate (and later professor of chemistry) Benjamin Silliman in 1801 created a Hindu character, Shacoolen, through whom he ventriloquized a variety of partisan opinions. Only later, when Silliman attended lectures on Asiatic diseases in Edinburgh in 1805, did he encounter a real "Hindu" and witness his reactions to the material presented on India.[25]

South Asians therefore functioned for white Americans as the new noble savages, far more to be admired than America's own native peoples and noteworthy for their cultures' clearly ancient roots. It is significant, in this regard, that Sir William Jones' *Asiatic Researches* was *not* the model for examinations of Native American languages. Again, admitting this comparison would confer too much dignity on America's aboriginal peoples. But so keen was Caleb Atwater (an Ohio lawyer interested in Native American antiquities) to find an ancient connection to India that he claimed the moundbuilders of the Ohio valley had originated there. These people, he believed, were later displaced by the ancestors of present-day Native Americans, migrants from Tartary who were incapable of the large-scale projects and urban life that the mound-builders had accomplished. It was left to United States citizens to re-establish the connection to India (and elliptically to the British empire) through exploration and

[49]

A comparative View of the Quadrupeds of Europe and of America.

I. *Aboriginals of both.*

	Europe.	America.
	lb.	lb.
Mammoth		
Buffalo. Bifon		*1800
White bear. Ours blanc		
Caribou. Renne		
Bear. Ours	153.7	*410
Elk. Elan. Original, palmated		
Red deer. Cerf	288.8	*273
Fallow deer. Daim	167.8	
Wolf. Loup	69.8	
Roe. Chevreuil	56.7	
Glutton. Glouton. Carcajou		
Wild cat. Chat fauvage		†30
Lynx. Loup cervier	25.	
Beaver. Caftor	18.5	*45
Badger. Blaireau	13.6	
Red fox. Renard	13.5	
Grey fox. Ifatis		
Otter. Loutre	8.9	†12
Monax. Marmotte	6.5	
Vifon. Fouine	2.8	
Hedgehog. Heriffon	2.2	
Marten. Marte	1.9	†6
	oz.	
Water rat. Rat d'eau	7.5	
Wefel. Belette	2.2	oz.
Flying fquirrel. Polatouche	2.2	†4
Shrew moufe. Mufaraigne	1.	

trade. As part of this curious effort, Lewis and Clark were instructed to seek out some route (via water or land) to the Pacific and thence to Asia. This, they did not find.[26]

If the United States remained apart from the Old World's ancient civilizations, perhaps its flora and fauna could demonstrate the nation's natural importance. All leading European arguments, however, were against it. Since the sixteenth century, Europeans had believed that the western hemisphere was newer than the eastern, therefore colder, damper, and less habitable. Its plants were primitive and shallowly rooted; its animals, small and timid. Georges Louis Leclerc, comte de Buffon, restated this opinion with particular force in the eighteenth century, and post-revolutionary citizens of the United States resented Buffon's thesis, fearful it implied that they too

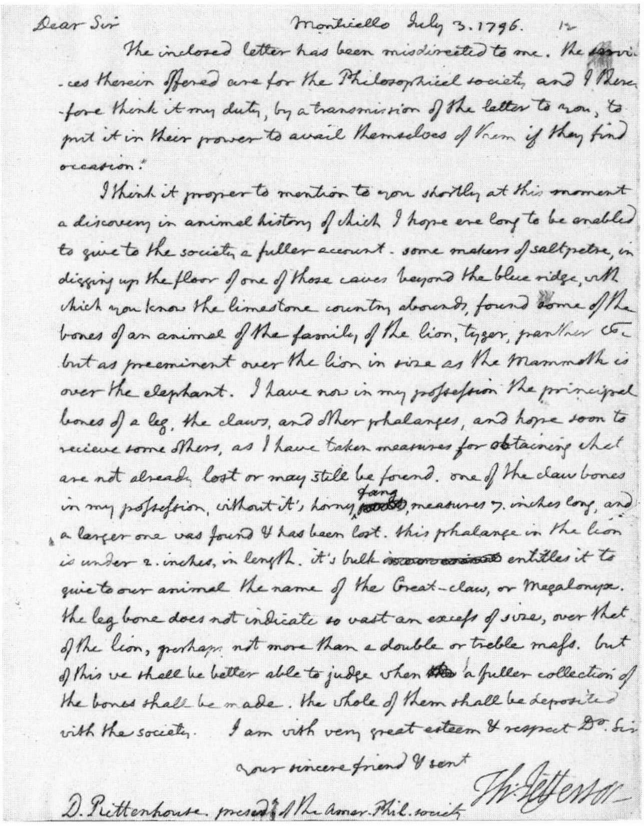

FIGURE 23 Thomas Jefferson, *Letter to David Rittenhouse, Monticello, July 3, 1796.* American Philosophical Society.

Dear Sir   Monticello July 3. 1796.   12

The inclosed letter has been misdirected to me. The services therein offered are for the Philosophical society, and I therefore think it my duty, by a transmission of the letter to you, to put it in their power to avail themselves of them if they find occasion.

I think it proper to mention to you shortly at this moment a discovery in animal history of which I hope ere long to be enabled to give to the society a fuller account. some makers of saltpetre, in digging up the floor of one of those caves beyond the blue ridge, with which you know the limestone country abounds, found some of the bones of an animal of the family of the lion, tiger, panther &c. but as preeminent over the lion in size as the mammoth is over the elephant. I have now in my possession the principal bones of a leg, the claws, and other phalanges, and hope soon to recieve some others, as I have taken measures for obtaining what are not already lost or may still be found. one of the claw bones in my possession, without it's horny tang measures 7. inches long, and a larger one was found & has been lost. this phalange in the lion is under 2. inches, in length. it's bulk entitles it to give to our animal the name of the Great-claw, or Megalonyx. the leg bone does not indicate so vast an excess of size, over that of the lion, perhaps not more than a double or treble mass. but of this we shall be better able to judge when a fuller collection of the bones shall be made. the whole of them shall be deposited with the society.   I am with very great esteem & respect Dr. Sir

your sincere friend & servt   Th: Jefferson

D. Rittenhouse. presdt of the Amer. Phil. society.

might be naturally deficient in body and spirit. Thomas Jefferson offered a spirited refutation in *Notes on the State of Virginia* (1784), which featured an elaborate table (FIGURE 22) comparing animals in the Old and New Worlds in order to demonstrate their largeness and variety in America.[27]

It was therefore tremendously exciting when Americans excavated many enormous animal bones during the late eighteenth century. Describing the "Great-claw, or Megalonyx," Jefferson emphasized with false modesty that "the leg bone does not indicate so vast an excess of size, over that of the lion, perhaps not more than a double or treble mass" (FIGURE 23). At first, Jefferson and others believed these specimens belonged to animals once extant on the eastern seaboard but still roaming out west; bones of the extinct mastodon were thought to be evidence of living mammoths. (Jefferson told Lewis and Clark to be on the lookout for them.) But as more and different kinds of these bones emerged (FIGURE 24), as no living creatures of such size were discovered, and as theories of animal extinction based on the work of French naturalist Georges Cuvier acquired authority, Americans sadly renounced dreams of discovering native animals to rival Old World elephants. In the process, however, they finally found antique foundations for their nation: fossils. By the early 1800s, the extinct mastodon became a nationalist symbol, evidence of North America's ancient and important natural history on which its new natives, the United States' white population, could build the lasting polity and society that they believed Native Americans had failed to construct.[28]

These debates over the nature of America interested the general public, not just an elite. Popularization of the sciences was a trade-off: if the United States lacked an aristocracy and a government willing to fund scientific pursuits, men of science had to court public opinion in order to earn money and get attention. For example, everyone from working men to wealthy matrons paid to attend John Griscom's chemical lectures in New York City in the early 1800s. These and even academic lectures necessarily stressed sensational rather than learned qualities. One poem on Griscom said he used

> Words to the witches in Macbeth unknown,
> Hydraulics, Hydrostatics, and Pneumatics...
> Also,—why frogs, for want of air, expire;
> And how to set the Tappan sea on fire.[29]

Benjamin Silliman's lectures on chemistry at Yale were evidently remarkable as "a constant appeal to the delighted senses. Here were broad irradiations of emerald phosphorescence. . . . Strange sounds saluted the ear."[30]

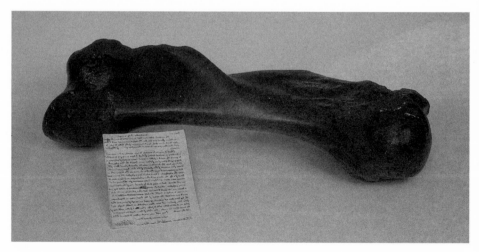

FIGURE 24 Thomas Jefferson, *Mastodon (Mammut americanum): Right Humerus.* Collected by William Clark at Big Bone Lick, Kentucky, 1807. American Philosophical Society, on deposit at the Academy of Natural Sciences of Philadelphia. With Jefferson's *Letter to David Rittenhouse, Monticello, July 3, 1796.* American Philosophical Society. Photograph by Will Brown.

Under these circumstances, it is not surprising that non-rational elements crept into American naturalists' work. To compare the United States to Britain is again revealing. One reason for the mystical character of natural history in the United States had to do with the place of religion in the states. It is not the case that more Americans than Britons were religious, or that religion and science were competing cultural impulses. But the manner in which American science and religion inflected each other was quite different from the situation in Britain, and this had everything to do with the legally sanctioned religious freedom in the new nation.

The United States had few if any curbs on public expression of religious dissent and it had no national religion—each state had its own laws regulating religion; several states had separated church and state; and a variety of religious ideas played across American culture. In England, by contrast, the Church of England remained the established religion, one that discouraged lay enthusiasm and heterodoxy; its formal presence at the two universities and influence in the Royal Society warned dissenters that their beliefs were not welcome in discussions of the sciences. Thus, the Methodists, who reacted strongly against Newtonianism and presented explanations of matter that combined spiritual with physical causes, operated outside the dominant sphere. Indeed, sectarian revivals in England were strongest among the poorer, less educated, and less powerful ranks in society, in contrast to the United States, where religious revivalism flourished in all classes.[31]

It was therefore difficult for Britons who had heterodox religious opinions to influence the natural sciences. For example, Joseph Priestley's religious and scientific (as well as political) views were decidedly radical. Priestley's criticism of established religion and his cheerful materialism were outside the mainstream; it was no small matter either to argue that the British state should have less power over religion *or* that human souls were composed of material particles, let alone both. Dubbed the "arch-priest of Pandaemonium liberty," Priestley endured infamy until 1791, when mobs in Birmingham destroyed his church, house, and laboratory. He fled to Pennsylvania where, in sharp contrast, his religion and science attracted little attention. In England, outsiders like William Blake would continue to be the ones who questioned natural science and promoted mystical views of the living creation; in America, those with radical sensibilities could define, in public, heterodox views of the creation.[32]

Heterodoxy was apparent, for example, in William Bartram's *Travels through North and South Carolina, Georgia, East and West Florida* (1791). Son of royal botanist John Bartram, William was a serious naturalist, but he used his natural history to explore nature as a sublime presence, a reminder of the inconsequential human place in the cosmos. Bartram's account of his botanizing expeditions emphasized the wonder and enormity of North America, and offered some Indian groups as examples of primordially harmonious communities. Indeed, the fantastic landscape he depicted exemplified desire to escape urban and industrial places as much as it recorded the physical features of the southeast (PLATE 12). Bartram's work in fact sold better in Europe than in America and would significantly influence romantic writers like Coleridge and Wordsworth; Coleridge's *Xanadu* was supposed to be inspired in part by Bartram's mystical southern landscape and alluring Cherokee maidens.[33]

A specifically American natural history was just emerging by the first decade of the nineteenth century. Colonists' participation in natural history had long been marked by a colonial relationship with Britain (and the rest of Europe); this connection continued even after the American Revolution, with Americans still acting mostly as consumers of Old World theories and producers of raw commodities in the form of specimens. While Americans dug up fossils, for example, it was Georges Cuvier who theorized the species extinction that made sense of these bones and would lead into later evolutionary theories about the origins of species, not least that of Charles Darwin. Still, citizens of the new republic were interested in demonstrating their intellectual abilities and the wonders of their natural world. Natural history provided a means toward these ends, even as conditions in the early republic favored small-scale, privately funded science that stressed to audiences its more sensational phenomena.

In texts like Bartram's *Travels*, emphasis on American nature's sublime qualities had surprising impact on European readers, surpassing that of more formally scientific enterprises such as those of Lewis and Clark or Alexander Wilson. The early republic's relative lack of support for learning and its tendency to stress unorthodox views of the natural world marked two generations of Americans. In the critical era when American nationalism focused on spreading a federal republic over a continent, an emphasis on American nature as overwhelming and mysterious emerged and would have lasting consequences. Assumptions about the vastness and mystery of nature would reappear, for instance, in sources as varied as the essays of Ralph Waldo Emerson (1803–1882) and the paintings of Fredrick Edwin Church (1826–1900). Thus did nature and nation give each other distinctive forms within the natural history of the early American republic.

Endnotes

1. Margaret C. Jacob, *The Newtonians and the English Revolution, 1689–1720* (Ithaca: Cornell University Press, 1976); D. G. C. Allan and R. E. Schofield, *Stephen Hales: Scientist and Philanthropist* (London: Scolar Press, 1980), 10–19, 30–64; John Gascoigne, *Cambridge in the Age of the Enlightenment: Science, Religion, and Politics from the Restoration to the French Revolution* (Cambridge: Cambridge University Press, 1989), 142–184; B. J. T. Dobbs, "Newton as Final Cause and First Mover," *Isis* 85 (1994): 633–643; Steven Shapin, *The Scientific Revolution* (Chicago: University of Chicago Press, 1996); Joyce E. Chaplin, "Mark Catesby, a Skeptical Newtonian in America," in Amy R. W. Meyers and Margaret Beck Pritchard, eds., *Empire's Nature: Mark Catesby's New World Vision* (Chapel Hill: University of North Carolina Press, 1998).

2. Otto Mayr, *Authority, Liberty, and Automatic Machinery in Early Modern Europe* (Baltimore: Johns Hopkins University Press, 1986); Gascoigne, 142–184.

3. Anthony Grafton, *New Worlds, Ancient Texts: The Power of Tradition and the Shock of Discovery* (Cambridge, MA: Harvard University Press), ch. 3; Frans A. Stafleu, *Linnaeus and the Linnaeans: The Spreading of Their Ideas in Systematic Botany, 1735–1789* (Utrecht: International Association for Plant Taxonomy, 1971).

4. Jan Golinski, *Science as Public Culture: Chemistry and Enlightenment in Britain, 1760–1820*, (Cambridge: Cambridge University Press, 1992); Ann B. Shteir, *Cultivating Women, Cultivating Science: Flora's Daughters and Botany in England, 1760 to 1860* (Baltimore: Johns Hopkins University Press, 1996); Fredrika J. Teute, "The Loves of the Plants; or, The Cross-Fertilization of Science and Desire at the End of the Eighteenth Century," *Huntington Library Quarterly* 63 (2000): 319–345.

5. I. Bernard Cohen, *Franklin and Newton: An Inquiry into Speculative Newtonian Experimental Science and Franklin's Work in Electricity as an Example Thereof* (Philadelphia: American Philosophical Society, 1956); Brooke Hindle, *The Pursuit of Science in Revolutionary America, 1735–1789* (Chapel Hill: University of North Carolina Press, 1956), 11–35; Raymond Phineas Stearns, *Science in the British Colonies of America* (Urbana: University of Illinois Press, 1970), chs. 5–10.

6. David R. Brigham, "Mark Catesby and the Patronage of Natural History in the First Half of the Eighteenth Century," in Meyers and Pritchard, eds.

7. Richard Harry Drayton, *Nature's Government: Science, Imperial Britain, and the "Improvement" of the World* (New Haven: Yale University Press, 2000).

8. Lucile Brockway, *Science and Colonial Expansion: The Role of the Royal Botanic Gardens* (New York: Academic Press, 1979); David I. Mackay, *In the Wake of Cook: Exploration, Science, and Empire, 1780–1801* (London: Croom Helm, 1985), esp. ch. 1; John Gascoigne, *Science in the Service of Empire: Joseph Banks, the British State and the Uses of Science in the Age of Revolution* (Cambridge: Cambridge University Press, 1998), 24–25, 128–46; David Philip Miller and Peter Hanns Reill, *Visions of Empire: Voyages, Botany, and Representations of Nature* (New York: Cambridge University Press, 1996); Drayton.

9. James E. McClellan, III, *Science Reorganized: Scientific Societies in the Eighteenth Century* (New York: Columbia University Press, 1985), 145–151; Simon Shaffer, "Experimenters' Techniques, Dyers' Hands, and the Electric Planetarium," *Isis* 88 (1997): 456–483; Margaret C. Jacob, *Scientific Culture and the Making of the Industrial West* (New York: Oxford University Press, 1997), ch. 4.

10. L. S. Jacyna, "Immanence or Transcendence: Theories of Organisation in Britain, 1790–1835," *Isis* 74 (1983): 311–329; Thomas L. Hankins, *Science and the Enlightenment* (Cambridge: Cambridge University Press, 1985), chs. 3, 5; Maureen McNeil, *Under the Banner of Science: Erasmus Darwin and His Age* (Manchester: Manchester University Press, 1987), ch. 4.

11. Erasmus Darwin, *Zoonomia; or, The Laws of Organic Life* (London: J. Johnson, 1794–1796), 467, 509; McNeil, 92–105; Jenny Uglow, *The Lunar Men: The Friends Who Made the Future* (London: Faber and Faber, 2002).

12. Mackay, ch. 5; Linda Colley, *Britons: Forging the Nation, 1707–1837* (New Haven: Yale University Press, 1992); Gascoigne, *Science in the Service of Empire*, ch. 7; Drayton, ch. 4.

13. Deepak Kumar, "The Evolution of Colonial Science in India: Natural History and the East India Company," in John MacKenzie, ed., *Imperialism and the Natural World* (Manchester: Manchester University Press, 1990); Richard H. Grove, *Green Imperialism: Colonial Expansion, Tropical Island Edens and the Origins of Environmentalism, 1600–1860* (New York: Cambridge University Press, 1995), esp. chs. 6–8; Matthew Edney, *Mapping an Empire: The Geographical Construction of British India, 1765–1843* (Chicago: University of Chicago Press, 1997); Alexander Murray, ed., *Sir William Jones, 1746–1794: A Commemoration* (Oxford: Oxford University Press, 1998).

14. Erasmus Darwin, *The Loves of the Plants* (1789), Canto I, lines 61–64.

15. Michael Adas, *Machines as the Measure of Man: Science, Technology, and Ideologies of Western Dominance* (Ithaca: Cornell University Press, 1989); Londa Schiebinger, *Nature's Body: Gender in the Making of Modern Science* (Boston: Beacon Press, 1993), 28–37.

16. John C. Greene, *American Science in the Age of Jefferson* (Ames: Iowa State University Press, 1984), chs. 2–5; McClellan, 140–145; Simon Baatz, "'Squinting at Silliman': Scientific Periodicals in the Early American Republic, 1810–1833," *Isis* 82 (1991): 223–244.

17. Greene, 396.

18. Greene, 139.

19. On the lack of a wealthy elite in the early United States, see Gordon S. Wood, *The Radicalism of the American Revolution: How a Revolution Transformed a Monarchical Society into a Democratic One Unlike Any That Had Ever Existed* (New York: A. A. Knopf, 1992), ch. 15.

20. Hindle, ch. 15; Greene 1984, chs. 6, 7 (backwardness), pp. 131, 144 (math).

21. Hindle, ch. 14; Greene, 11, 205–206.

22. Greene, chs. 8–11.

23. Laura Rigal, *The American Manufactory: Art, Labor, and the World of Things in the Early Republic* (Princeton: Princeton University Press, 1998), ch. 5.

24. Greene, 213, ch. 14; Edward G. Gray, *New World Babel: Languages and Nations in Early America* (Princeton: Princeton University Press, 1999), 116–118.

25. Chandos Michael Brown, *Benjamin Silliman: A Life in the Young Republic* (Princeton: Princeton University Press, 1989), 71–83, 188.

26. Robert A. Ferguson, "The Emulation of Sir William Jones in the Early Republic," *New England Quarterly* 52 (1979): 1–26; Greene, 196–199 (passage to Pacific), 366–369 (Atwater); Gray, 116–118.

27. Antonello Gerbi, *The Dispute of the New World: The History of a Polemic, 1750–1900*, trans. Jeremy Moyle (Pittsburgh: Pittsburgh University Press, 1973), chs. 1–5.

28. Paul Semonin, *American Monster: How the Nation's First Prehistoric Creature Became a Symbol of National Identity* (New York: New York University Press, 2000).

29. Greene, 25.

30. Greene, 179. On the public nature of American sciences, see Greene, 20–27.

31. E. P. Thompson, *The Making of the English Working Class* (New York: Vintage Books, 1966), ch. 11; Jacob, *Newtonians*, ch. 7; Wood, 329–334; Peter Lineham, "Methodism and Popular Science in the Enlightenment," *Enlightenment and Dissent* 17 (1998): 104–125; John Gascoigne, "Science, Religion, and the Foundations of Morality in Enlightenment Britain," *Enlightenment and Dissent* 17 (1998): 83–103.

32. E. P. Thompson, *Witness against the Beast: William Blake and the Moral Law* (New York: Cambridge University Press, 1993); Robert E. Schofield, *The Enlightenment of Joseph Priestley* (Philadelphia: University of Pennsylvania Press, 1997); Uglow, 437–443, 459–460.

33. John Livingston Lowes, *The Road to Xanadu: A Study in the Ways of the Imagination* (Boston: Houghton Mifflin, 1927); Greene, 277–280; Duncan Wu, *Wordsworth's Reading, 1770–1790* (Cambridge: Cambridge University Press, 1993); Duncan Wu, *Wordsworth's Reading, 1800–1815* (Cambridge: Cambridge University Press, 1995).

Selected Bibliography

The following list includes major secondary sources used by the authors in their essays. For primary sources and for more extensive secondary source material, please see the notes at the end of each chapter.

Altick, Richard D. *The Shows of London*. Cambridge, MA: Harvard University Press, 1978.

Bartram, William. *Travels and Other Writings*. Thomas P. Slaughter, ed. New York: Library of America, 1996.

Boorstin, Daniel J. *The Lost World of Thomas Jefferson*. Boston: Beacon Press, 1948.

Catesby, Mark. *The Natural History of Carolina, Florida and the Bahama Islands*. 2 vols. London: Charles Marsh, Thomas Wilcox, and Benjamin Stichall, 1754.

Dance, S. Peter. *Shell Collecting: An Illustrated History*. Berkeley: University of California Press, 1966.

Donovan, Edward. *Instructions for Collecting and Preserving Various Subjects of Natural History*. London: privately printed, 1794.

Fliegelman, Jay. *Declaring Independence: Jefferson, Natural Language, and the Culture of Performance*. Stanford: Stanford University Press, 1993.

Foucault, Michel. *The Order of Things: An Archaeology of the Human Sciences*. New York: Vintage Books, 1970.

Gascoigne, John. *Science in the Service of Empire: Joseph Banks, the British State and the Uses of Science in the Age of Revolution*. Cambridge: Cambridge University Press, 1998.

Greene, John C. *American Science in the Age of Jefferson*. Ames: Iowa State University Press, 1984.

Gunther, R.T. *Early Science in Oxford*. Oxford: Oxford University Press, 1925.

Hindle, Brooke. *The Pursuit of Science in Revolutionary America, 1735–1789*. Chapel Hill: University of North Carolina Press, 1956.

Impey, Oliver, and Arthur MacGregor, eds. *The Origin of Museums: The Cabinet of Curiosities in Sixteenth and Seventeenth Century Europe*. Oxford: Clarendon Press, 1985.

Jacob, Margaret C. *Scientific Culture and the Making of the Industrial West*. New York: Oxford University Press, 1997.

Looby, Christopher. "The Constitution of Nature: Taxonomy as Politics in Jefferson, Peale, and Bartram." *Early American Literature* 22 (1987): 252–273.

Meyers, Amy R.W., and Margaret Beck Pritchard, eds. *Empire's Nature: Mark Catesby's New World Vision*. Chapel Hill: University of North Carolina Press, 1998.

Miller, Lillian B. *The Selected Papers of Charles Willson Peale*, vol. 2. New Haven: Yale University Press, 1988.

Potts, Alex. "Natural Order and the Call of the Wild: the Politics of Animal Picturing." *The Oxford Art Journal* 13, (1) (1990): 12–33.

Sellers, Charles Coleman. *Mr. Peale's Museum*. New York: W. W. Norton, 1980.

Stearns, Raymond Phineas. *Science in the British Colonies of America*. Urbana and Chicago: University of Illinois Press, 1970.

Checklist of the Exhibition

Jane E. Boyd

Items are first listed alphabetically by artist, author, or principal collector, with anonymous works at the beginning. Under each person's name, items occur in the following order, if present: portraits, natural history specimens (with fieldworker's name, if applicable), drawings and prints, manuscripts and letters, and books and other printed materials.

Plant and animal specimens are then listed by their current common names, with current scientific names in parentheses. Other names assigned by the original collectors, if known, are given in quotation marks and parentheses. Likewise, where exact identification is possible, pictures of plants and animals are listed by their current common names, with current scientific names in parentheses. Other names inscribed on the drawing or print are given in parentheses and quotation marks, although inscriptions are abbreviated.

For published books and pamphlets, titles have been truncated, capitalization of titles has been regularized, place names have been anglicized, and publishers' names have been standardized. Manuscripts that are not letters (i.e., bound manuscript volumes or papers that have specific titles) are marked (MS) to distinguish them from published works. Dimensions of paintings, drawings, prints, and broadsides are given to the nearest eighth of an inch. Items illustrated in this catalogue are marked with an asterisk (*).

Lenders to the Exhibition (with abbreviations used in checklist)

All objects exhibited belong to the American Philosophical Society (APS) unless otherwise noted.

ANSP	The Academy of Natural Sciences of Philadelphia
ANSP-L	The Academy of Natural Sciences of Philadelphia, Ewell Sale Stewart Library
APS at ANSP	American Philosophical Society, on deposit at the Academy of Natural Sciences of Philadelphia
DIA	The Detroit Institute of Arts
EML	Ernst Mayr Library of the Museum of Comparative Zoology, Harvard University
GH	Archives of the Gray Herbarium, Harvard University
INHP	Independence National Historical Park
LCP	The Library Company of Philadelphia
MCZ	Museum of Comparative Zoology, Harvard University
PHS at APS	Pennsylvania Horticultural Society, on deposit at the American Philosophical Society
PML	The Pierpont Morgan Library, New York
UPENN	Annenberg Rare Book and Manuscript Library, University of Pennsylvania
RYSKAMP	Charles Ryskamp, New York
WLC	William L. Clements Library, University of Michigan

Collections

ALS   Alexander Lawson Scrapbooks, The Academy of Natural Sciences of Philadelphia, Ewell Sale Stewart Library

BDC   Barton-Delafield Collection (Benjamin Smith Barton Papers: The Violetta W. Delafield Collection), APS

Artist unknown

Elk Skeleton, n.d, Etching, 19 3/4 x 13 1/2 in. BDC

Author unknown

Amusement here with Science is combin'd, To please, improve, and cultivate the mind, n.d. Collage, 13 7/8 x 9 1/4 in.

Elementary Reading Book in Ojibway: Old Testament Bible Stories, Story of Joseph, and Natural History (Kishemanito Muzinaigun Tezhiuindumiin...). Boston: Crocker and Brewster, 1835.

Great American Mastodon!! Now Exhibiting at the Hall..., 1845 or 1846. Broadside, 25 1/4 x 17 3/4 in.

Just Arrived!!! A Great Serpent, from America.... London: Schulze and Dean, 1818. Broadside, 11 1/8 x 8 3/4 in.

Collector unknown

Common Map Turtle (Graptemys geographica). Collected in New York, 1820. ANSP

Longnose Gar (Lepisosteus osseus). Collected in the Delaware River at Trenton, New Jersey, ca. 1859. ANSP

Snout of Sawfish (Pristis antiquorum). Collected 19th c. ANSP

White-Tailed Tropicbird Skeleton (Phaethon lepturus). Collected in the Indian Ocean near Mauritius, ca. 1852. MCZ

Maker unknown

Materials and Tools for Taxidermy: Ceramic Teeth, Glass Eyes (some hand-painted), Mortar and Pestle, Modeling Tool, Wax and Modeling Carver, Fleshing Beam, and Pinning Needle, 19th or early 20th c. ANSP

Agassiz, Louis (1807–1873)

John Sartain. *Portrait of Louis Agassiz*, n.d. Mezzotint and engraving, 8 7/8 x 5 7/8 in.

With Augustus A. Gould (1805–1866). *Principles of Zoology...Part I. Comparative Physiology*. Boston: Gould, Kendall and Lincoln, 1848.

Audubon, John James (1785–1851)

Engraver unknown, after Alonzo Chappel. *Portrait of John J. Audubon*, 1861. Engraving, 11 x 8 1/2 in.

Fox Squirrel (Sciurus niger). Collected in the southeastern United States, n.d. ANSP

Two Northern Flickers (Colaptes auratus) (one labeled "Colaptes hybridus"). Probably collected by Edward Harris near Fort Union Trading Post, Williston, North Dakota, summer 1843. ANSP

Green Woodpecker (Picus viridis) ("Le Pic Vert"), 1805. Pastel, graphite, and ink, 18 3/8 x 12 1/8 in. MCZ

Ruffed Grouse (Bonasa umbellus), ca. 1810. Graphite and colored chalks, 15 1/2 x 20 in. EML

Baily, William L. (1828–1861)

"Illustrations of the Trochilidae, or Hummingbirds," vol. 1, 1855–1858. Watercolor, opaque pigment, and graphite, highlighted with gold leaf. ANSP-L

Barton, Benjamin Smith
(1766–1815)

Charles Balthazar Julien Fevret de Saint-Mémin. *Portrait of Benjamin Smith Barton*, 1802. Engraving, 2 1/4 in. diameter.

Herbarium, vol. 2, 1795. Plant specimens in bound volume. ANSP [Figure 10, this catalogue]

Red Algae (genus Gracilaria?) ("*Fucus conferva*"), nos. 10, 11, and 12. Possibly collected by Frederick Pursh, n.d. BDC

Badger (Taxidea taxus), n.d. Watercolor and graphite, 13 5/8 x 16 3/8 in. BDC

Florida Anise-Tree Flower (Illicium floridanum), ca. 1800. Watercolor, gouache, graphite, and ink, 8 1/2 x 11 7/8 in. BDC

Fungal Sporophore, n.d. Watercolor, graphite, and ink, 8 7/8 x 9 in. BDC

Fungi, n.d. Attributed to B. S. Barton. Watercolor, graphite, and ink, 14 5/8 x 10 3/4 in. BDC

Greater Siren (Siren lacertina), n.d. Watercolor and graphite, 12 5/8 x 18 in. BDC

Hellbender (Salamander) (Cryptobranchus alleganiensis), ca. 1812. Grisaille watercolor and graphite with white bodycolor, 9 3/4 x 15 1/8 in. BDC

Hellbender, ca. 1812. Watercolor, 12 x 19 1/2 in. BDC

Hellbender, ca. 1812. Copper engraving plate, 5 1/8 x 9 1/2 in. BDC

Hellbender, ca. 1812. Two proof engravings, 6 x 9 5/8 in. and 5 1/2 x 9 1/4 in. BDC

Jimsonweed Flower (Datura stramonium), n.d. Watercolor and graphite, 8 7/8 x 11 1/4 in. BDC

Lily Flower (family Liliaceae), possibly from William Hamilton's "Stove" or Hothouse, n.d. Watercolor, graphite, and gouache, 11 5/8 x 18 3/8 in. BDC

Native American Petroglyphs or Pictographs, n.d. Ink, 4 x 6 3/8 in. BDC

Northern Short-Tailed Shrew? (Blarina brevicauda) with House in Background (catalogued as "Mole"), n.d. Watercolor, graphite, and ink, 16 1/2 x 11 in. BDC

Walrus Skull and Dugong Skull (Odobenus rosmarus and Dugong dugon) ("Trichechi rosmari...Trichechi dugong"), n.d. Watercolor, graphite, and ink, 8 5/8 x 10 1/4 in. BDC

Queries Concerning Native Americans ("...sent, March 25th, 1806, to Mr. J. Parish, of Cananda[i]gua"), 1806 (MS). BDC

*Elements of Botany; or, Outlines of the Natural History of Vegetables...*2 vols. Philadelphia: Printed for the author, 1803.

A Memoir Concerning an Animal of the Class of Reptilia, or Amphibia, which is known, in the United-States, by the Names of Alligator and Hell-Bender. Philadelphia: Griggs and Dickinson, 1812.

A Memoir Concerning the Fascinating Faculty which has been Ascribed to the Rattle-Snake, and Other American Serpents. Philadelphia: Henry Sweitzer, 1796.

Bartram, John (1699–1777)

Map of the Middle Atlantic States, Showing Rivers and Mountains and Locations of Sea Shells on Mountaintops, ca. 1750–1760. Ink and graphite, 12 x 14 5/8 in.

Observations...Made by Mr. John Bartram, in his Travels from Pensilvania to Onondago, Oswego and the Lake Ontario, in Canada.... London: J. Whiston and B. White, 1751.

Bartram, William (1739–1823)

Charles Willson Peale. *Portrait of William Bartram*, ca. 1808 (facsimile exhibited). Oil on paper on canvas, 23 1/2 x 19 1/2 in. INHP

*Carolina Spiderlily
(Hymenocallis caroliniana), n.d.
Brown ink, 12 1/4 x 6 1/4 in.
BDC [Figure 13, this catalogue]

Common or Eastern Persimmon
(Diospyros virginiana), n.d.
Brown ink and watercolor,
10 3/8 x 7 1/8 in. BDC

Curly Virginsbower or Swamp
Leather Flower (Clematis crispa),
n.d. Brown ink, 10 5/8 x
8 1/4 in. BDC

Eastern Leatherwood or
Moosewood and Whorled
Pogonia or Purple Fiveleaf
Orchid (Dirca palustria and
Isotria verticillata) ("Dirca
palustris...Arethusa mediola"),
n.d. Brown ink, 9 7/8 x
7 5/8 in. BDC

Franklinia or Franklin Tree
(Franklinia alatamaha), n.d.
Hand-colored engraving by
James Trenchard, 11 7/8 x
9 5/8 in. BDC

*"The Great Alachua-Savana in
East Florida...," n.d. Brown and
black ink, 12 3/4 x 15 7/8 in.
BDC [Plate 12, this catalogue]

"Mico-chlucco, King of the
Muscogulges or Cricks, call'd the
Long Warrior," n.d. Watercolor,
graphite, and ink, 7 5/8 x
5 1/4 in. BDC

Oak (genus Quercus) ("Quercus
pennsylvanica .s. heterophylla"),
n.d. Brown ink, 10 1/2 x
8 1/4 in. BDC

Orangegrass or Pinweed
St. Johnswort (Hypericum
gentianoides) and Wood Frog
(Rana sylvatica) ("Sarothra
gentianoides...Ground Pine
...Rana"), 1794. Brown ink
and watercolor, 10 3/4 x
14 7/8 in. BDC

Red Bartsia (Odontites vernus)
("Bartsia coccinea"), 1801.
Brown ink and watercolor,
12 3/4 x 7 7/8 in. BDC

*Rosebud Orchid, Whorled
Pogonia or Purple Fiveleaf
Orchid, Venus Flytrap, and
Round-Leaf Sundew, with
Philadelphia (?) in Background
(Cleistes divaricata, Isotria
verticillata, Dionea muscipula,
Drosera rotundifolia) ("Arethusa
divaricata..."), 1796. Brown ink,
14 3/4 x 8 3/4 in. BDC [Plate 11,
this catalogue]

Purple Pitcherplant (Sarracenia
purpurea), n.d. Brown ink,
9 7/8 x 7 5/8 in. BDC

*Red Canna or Indian Shot
(Canna indica), 1784. Brown
ink, 10 5/8 x 8 1/4 in. BDC
[Figure 17, this catalogue]

Scentless Mock-Orange
(Philadelphus inodorus), n.d.
Brown ink, 9 7/8 x 5 1/8 in. BDC

Spiny Softshell Turtle (Apalone
spinifera) ("The soft shell'd
Tortoise got in Savanah River
Georgia"), May 1773. Brush
and gray and black wash, over
graphite, 3 3/8 x 14 15/16 in.
RYSKAMP

Watershield (Brasenia schreberi),
1800. Brown ink, 9 7/8 x
15 1/4 in. BDC

Whorled Pogonia or Purple
Fiveleaf Orchid? (Isotria
verticillata) ("Arethusa super-
ba...Arethusa medeola"), n.d.
Brown ink, 10 x 7 5/8 in. BDC

Wood Turtle (Clemmys insculp-
ta) ("Testudo calata"), n.d. Ink,
8 1/8 x 10 5/8 in. BDC

Travels through North & South
Carolina, Georgia, East & West
Florida.... Philadelphia: James
and Johnson, 1791.

Bigland, John (1750–1832)

A Natural History of Animals....
Philadelphia: John Grigg, 1832.

Bonaparte, Charles Lucien
(1803–1857)

Two Common Guitarfish
(Rhinobatos rhinobatos)
("Rhinobatus columnae").
Collected in the Mediterranean
Sea near Italy, ca. 1830–1836.
ANSP

Five European Sturgeons
(Acipenser sturio). Attributed
to C. L. Bonaparte. Collected
in the Mediterranean Sea,
ca. 1830–1846.

"Rudd" Minnow (Leuciscus
scardafa). Collected in the lakes
of Italy, ca. 1830–1837. ANSP

Observations on the Nomenclature of Wilson's Ornithology. Philadelphia: Finley, 1826.

Budgen, L. M. (Miss)

Episodes of Insect Life; by Acheta Domestica, M. E. S., third series, vol. 3. New York: J. S. Redfield..., 1851.

Buffon, Georges Louis Leclerc, comte de (1707–1788)

Amédée Félix Barthélémy Geille, after Pierre J. Lion. *Portrait of George Louis Leclerc, comte de Buffon,* n.d. Hand-colored etching and engraving, 10 3/4 x 7 in.

Histoire naturelle, générale et particulière, avec la description du Cabinet du Roy. Tome premier. Paris: De l'Imprimerie royale, 1749.

Histoire naturelle, générale et particulière...Quadrupèdes, Tome troisième. Paris: De l'Imprimerie royale, 1784.

Histoire naturelle, générale et particulière...Nouvelle édition, vol. 28. Paris: De l'Imprimerie de F. Dufart, 1799–1800.

Catesby, Mark (1683–1749)

Manuscript Entries for Appendix, vol. 2 of The Natural History of Carolina, Florida, and the Bahama Islands..., n.d. PML

*The Natural History of Carolina, Florida, and the Bahama Islands..., vol. 2 (2nd ed.). London: C. Marsh..., 1754. PHS at APS [Plate 9 and Figure 12, this catalogue]

Colden, Cadwallader (1688–1776)

Mathew Pratt, after P. Purdon Graham. *Portrait of Lieut. Gov. Cadwallader Colden,* n.d. Engraving, 10 1/2 x 7 1/4 in.

*Plantae Coldenghamiae in Provincia Noveboracensi Americes sponte crescentes, quas ad methodum Cl. Linnaei sexualem, anno 1742 &c. Uppsala, 1749. [Figure 19, this catalogue]

Colman, Pamela Atkins, ed. (1824–1900)

Boys' and Girls' Magazine, vols. 1–3 (Jan.–Dec. 1843). Boston: T. H. Carter, 1843.

Comstock, John Lee (1789–1858)

The Young Botanist: Being a Treatise on the Science, Prepared for the Use of Persons just Commencing the Study of Plants. New York: Robinson, Pratt, 1835.

Correia da Serra, José Francisco (1750–1823)

Reduction of all the Genera of Plants contained in the Catalogus Plantarum Americae Septentrionalis, of the late Dr. Muhlenberg, to the Natural Families of Mr. de Jussieu's System.... Philadelphia: Solomon W. Conrad, 1815.

Cusick, David (d. ca. 1840)

David Cusick's Sketches of Ancient History of the Six Nations.... Lockport, New York: Turner and McCollum, 1848.

Cuvier, Georges, baron (1769–1832)

Antoine Joseph Chollet, after Mme. Lizinska Aimée Zoé de Mirbel and Antoine Cosme Giraud. *Portrait of Georges Cuvier,* n.d. Hand-colored etching and engraving, 10 3/4 x 6 7/8 in.

*Tableau élémentaire de l'histoire
naturelle des animaux*.... Paris:
Baudouin, 1798.

Darwin, Charles (1809–1882)

Thomas Herbert Maguire.
Portrait of Charles Darwin,
1849 (facsimile exhibited).
Lithograph, 11 1/2 x 9 5/8 in.

*Letter to Charles Lyell, Down,
Bromley, Kent, March 28, 1859,
enclosing Manuscript Draft
of Title Page of* On the Origin
of Species *("An abstract of an
Essay on the Origin of Species
and Varieties Through Natural
Selection...").*

Darwin, Erasmus (1731–1802)

*The Temple of Nature; or,
The Origin of Society: A Poem*....
New York: T. and J. Swords,
1804.

Dickeson, Montroville Wilson
(1810–1882)

*Indian Antiquities. A Course
of Popular and Highly
Interesting Lectures on American
Archaeology*.... Philadelphia:
Harris, n.d. Broadside, 16 1/8 x
7 1/2 in.

*Monumental Grandeur of the
Mississippi Valley! Now
Exhibiting for a Short Time
Only, With Scientific Lectures
on American Æerchiology*....
Newark, New Jersey: Mercury
Office, n.d. Broadside, 20 3/4 x
7 3/4 in.

Edgerton

*Scientific Lecture. Prof. Edgerton
of Michigan has the Pleasure
of Announcing...,* ca. 1840.
Broadside, 15 1/2 x 7 5/8 in.

Ellis, John (1710?–1776)

**Directions for Bringing Over
Seeds and Plants, from the
East-Indies and Other Distant
Countries, in a State of
Vegetation*.... London: L. Davis,
1770. PHS at APS [Figure 9, this
catalogue]

Geoffroy Saint-Hilaire, Etienne
(1772–1844)

*Philosophie anatomique:
Des organes respiratoires...Atlas.*
Paris: Méquignon-Marvis, 1818.

Godman, John Davidson
(1794–1830)

American Natural History,
vol. 3 (2nd ed.). Philadelphia:
Stoddart and Atherton, 1831.

Gray, Asa (1810–1888)

J. J. Cade. *Portrait of Prof. Asa
Gray, Harvard University,* n.d.
Engraving, 7 1/4 x 4 7/8 in.

*How Plants Grow: A Simple
Introduction to Structural
Botany*.... New York: Ivison
and Phinney, 1862.

Hale, Sarah Josepha Buell
(1788–1879)

*Flora's Interpreter: Or The
American Book of Flowers and
Sentiments.* 2nd ed. Boston:
Marsh, Capen and Lyon, 1832
[1833]. UPENN

*Flora's Interpreter: Or, the
American Book of Flowers and
Sentiments.* 5th ed. Boston:
Marsh, Capen and Lyon, 1836.
UPENN

Hall, O. A.

*A Brief Treatise on Astronomy,
Entomology, and General
Science*.... Lowell, [Massachu-
setts]: A. Watson, 1841.

**Heckewelder, John Gottlieb
Ernestus** (1743–1823)

*"Names of Various Trees, Shrubs
& Plants in the Language of
the Lennape..."* (MS), ca. 1820.

"Names Which the Lenni Lenape...Had Given to Rivers, Streams, Places, &c." (MS), 1822.

Hering, Constantine (1800–1880)

Bushmaster or Surucucu (Lachesis trigonocephalus). Collected in Suriname (formerly Surinam), July 28, 1828. ANSP

False Vampire Bat (Vampyrum spectrum). Collected in Suriname (formerly Surinam), ca. 1827–1833. ANSP

Holbrook, John Edwards (1794–1871)

Timber Rattlesnake (Crotalus horridus horridus). Collected in South Carolina, mid-19th c. ANSP

Warsaw Grouper (Epinephelus nigritus) ("Serranus nigritus"). Collected in Charleston, South Carolina, 1855. ANSP

Ichthyology of South Carolina. Charleston, South Carolina: Russell and Jones, 1860.

North American Herpetology; or, a Description of the Reptiles Inhabiting the United States, vol. 3. Philadelphia: J. Dobson, 1842.

Humphrey, George

*"Directions for Collecting and Preserving all kinds of Natural Curiosities, particularly Insects and Shells..." (MS), 1776. ANSP-L [Figure 4, this catalogue]

Hyrtl, Joseph (1811–1894)

Queen Triggerfish (Balistes vetula). Collected in the Antilles, ca. 1850. ANSP

Ingpen, Abel (d. 1854)

*Instructions for Collecting, Rearing, and Preserving British & Foreign Insects.... London: William Smith, 1839. ANSP-L [Plate 6, this catalogue]

Jacquin, Nikolaus Joseph, Freiherr von (1727–1817)

Selectarum Stirpium Americanarum Historia.... Vienna: Kraus, 1763. PHS at APS

Jefferson, Thomas (1743–1826)

Henry Bryan Hall, after Gilbert Stuart. Portrait of Thomas Jefferson, n.d. Engraving, 9 1/4 x 5 3/4 in.

Ancient Bison (Bison antiquus): Partial Skull and Toe Bones. Collected by William Clark at Big Bone Lick, Kentucky, 1807. APS at ANSP

Jefferson's Giant Ground Sloth (Megalonyx jeffersonii): Ulna and Radius of Forearm; Claws and Bones of Front Foot. Collected in Greenbrier County, West Virginia, 1796. APS at ANSP

*Mastodon (Mammut americanum): Right Humerus, Mandible, and Two Sets of Teeth with Roots. Collected by William Clark at Big Bone Lick, Kentucky, 1807. APS at ANSP [Figure 24, this catalogue]

*Comparative Vocabulary of Native American Languages: Leaf with List of Languages and Names for Turtledove (?), Pheasant, and Partridge (MS), 1802–1808. [Figure 21, this catalogue]

*Letter to David Rittenhouse (APS President), Monticello, July 3, 1796, Announcing Discovery of Megalonyx Bones. [Figure 23, this catalogue]

"A Memoir on the Discovery of certain Bones of a Quadruped of the Clawed Kind...." Transactions of the APS, vol. 4 (old series), 1799.

Notes on the State of Virginia; Written...for the Use of a Foreigner of Distinction, in Answer to Certain Queries Proposed by Him.... Paris: Philippe-Denis Pierres, 1784. [Figure 22, this catalogue]

Jussieu, Antoine-Laurent de (1748–1836)

"*Catalogue des plantes demon-treés en 1782 au Jardin du Roy*" (MS), 1783.

Jussieu, Bernard de (1699–1777)

Eustache Hyacinthe Langlois, after Armand Guilleminot. *Portrait of Bernard de Jussieu,* n.d. Hand-colored etching and engraving, 10 1/4 x 7 in.

Kalm, Pehr (1716–1779)

Travels into North America: Containing its Natural History..., vol. 2. Warrington: William Eyres, 1770–1771.

Kirby, R. S.

Kirby's Wonderful and Eccentric Museum, vol. 5. London: R. S. Kirby, 1815.

Koch, Albert C. (1804–1867)

Missourium Theristrocaulodon, or Leviathan Missouriensus open for Exhibition.... Dublin: C. Crookes, ca. 1841. Broadside, 9 7/8 x 7 3/8 in.

Lamarck, Jean Baptiste Pierre Antoine de Monet de (1744–1829)

Système des animaux sans vertèbres.... Paris: Deterville, 1801.

Latrobe, Benjamin Henry (1764–1820)

*Rattlesnake Skeleton (genus Crotalus), n.d. Attributed to Latrobe; formerly attributed to B. S. Barton. Watercolor, graphite, and glaze, 14 3/4 x 40 1/4 in. [Plate 10, this catalogue]

Four Rattlesnake Dissection Studies (genus Crotalus), n.d. Watercolor, graphite, and ink. *Anatomy of the Tail,* 6 1/4 x 13 3/4 in.; *Internal Organs,* 7 1/2 x 19 1/2 in.; *Organs of Generation,* 7 x 19 1/2 in.; *Muscles of the Scuta,* 6 1/4 x 13 1/2 in.

Lavater, Johann Caspar (1741–1801)

Johann Heinrich Lips. *Portrait of Johann Caspar Lavater,* n.d. Engraving, 8 1/4 x 6 1/2 in.

Regole fisonomiche o sia osser-vazioni della umana razza con quella de'bruti di Lavater.... Milan: Pietro and Giuseppe Vallardi, 1820.

LeConte, John Eatton (1784–1860)

Silver-Haired Bat (Lasionycteris noctivagans). Collected before 1861. ANSP

Entomological Drawings: Beetles (order Coleoptera), vol. 5, p. 53, n.d. Watercolor and graphite, 12 3/4 x 8 1/2 in (page dimensions).

Lettsom, John Coakley (1744–1815)

The Naturalist's and Traveller's Companion; Containing Instructions for Collecting and Preserving Objects of Natural History.... London: C. Dilly, 1799.

Lewis, Meriwether (1774–1809) and **William Clark** (1770–1838)

*Arrowleaf Balsamroot (Balsamorhiza sagittata). Two specimens, collected by Lewis in Lewis and Clark Pass, Montana, July 7, 1806, and by Clark along the Columbia River in Skamania or Klickitat County, Washington, April 14, 1806. APS at ANSP [Figure 11, this catalogue]

Curlycup Gumweed (Grindelia squarrosa). Collected at Tonwontonga (Omaha Indian town), Dakota County, Nebraska, August 17, 1804. APS at ANSP

Hollyleaved Barberry (Mahonia or Berberis aquifolium). Collected along the Columbia River, probably in Hood River County, Oregon, April 11, 1806. APS at ANSP

Lewis's Mock Orange (Philadelphus lewisii). Two specimens, collected by Lewis along the Clearwater River in Nez Perce County, Idaho, May 6, 1806, and along the Clark Fork, Missoula County, Montana, July 4, 1806. APS at ANSP

Silvery Lupine (Lupinus argenteus). Collected by Lewis in Lewis and Clark Pass, Montana, July 7, 1806. APS at ANSP

Spinulose Wood Fern (Dryopteris carthusiana). Collected at Fort Clatsop near Astoria, Oregon, January 20, 1806. APS at ANSP

Linnaean Society of New England

Report of a Committee...Relative to a Large Marine Animal, Supposed to be a Serpent.... Boston: Cummings and Hillyard..., 1817.

Linné, Carl von (Carolus Linnaeus) (1707–1778)

Friedrich August Andorf. *Portrait of Linnaeus in Laplander Costume*, n.d. Engraving, 9 1/2 x 8 1/2 in.

Pink Convolvulus (Convolvulus cantabrica). Collected ca. 1753 and sent to Linnaeus. ANSP

Classes Plantarum seu Systema Plantarum...Pars II. Leiden: Conradum Wishoff, 1738.

Materia Medica, Liber I: De Plantis Digestis Secundum.... Amsterdam: J. Wetstenium, 1749.

Systema Naturae, sive Regna Tria Naturae Systematice Proposita per Classes, Ordines, Genera, & Species. Leiden: Theodorum Haak, 1735. ANSP-L

Marshall, Humphry (1722–1801)

Arbustrum Americanum: The American Grove.... Philadelphia: Joseph Crukshank, 1785.

Melsheimer, Frederick Valentine (1749–1814)

A Catalogue of Insects of Pennsylvania. Hanover, Pennsylvania: W. D. Lepper, 1806.

Miami, Pottawattamie, Chippewa, and Wyandot Leaders

Letter to President James Madison Protesting Dishonest Agents, November 13, 1811. Exhibited: last page, with pictographic signatures. WLC

Michaux, André (1746–1802)

Five Packets of Seed Specimens: Ash (genus Fraxinus); Hazelnut (genus Corylus), from New York; Safflower (Carthamus tinctorius); Swamp Cyrilla (Cyrilla racemiflora), two packets, one from South Carolina. All collected in 1786. ANSP

Flora Boreali-Americana, Sistens Caracteres Plantarum quas in America septentrionali collegit et detexit Andreas Michaux..., vol. 1. Paris: Levrault, 1803. PHS at APS

Michaux, François André (1770–1855)

Henry Bryan Hall, after Rembrandt Peale. *Portrait of F. Andrew Michaux*, n.d. Engraving, 11 x 7 1/8 in.

Muhlenberg, Henry (1753–1815)

Western Twinflower (Linnaea borealis) ("Linnaea"). Date of collection unknown. ANSP

Catalogus Plantarum Americae Septentrionalis.... Lancaster, Pennsylvania: William Hamilton, 1813.

Nuttall, Thomas (1786–1859)

The Genera of North American Plants and a Catalogue of the Species to the Year 1817..., vol. 1. Philadelphia: D. Heartt, 1818.

Owen, Charles (d. 1746)

An Essay Towards a Natural History of Serpents.... London: Printed for the author, 1742.

Palisot de Beauvois, Ambroise Marie François Joseph (1752–1820)

Bald-Faced Hornets (Dolichovespula or Vespa maculata) and Nest ("The Hive of The Wasp call'd Vespa Maculata, from pensilvania near Philadelphia"), 1792. Watercolor and ink, 9 7/8 x 7 3/4 in. BDC

"Memoir on Amphibia: Serpents," Transactions of the APS, vol. 4 (old series), 1799.

Parker, Nicholas H.

Indian Historical Lectures, by Ga-I-Wah-Go-Wa.... Canandaigua, New York: Ontario Messenger Office, 1853. Broadside, 12 1/4 x 5 3/4 in.

Patterson, Robert Maskell (1787–1854)

Three Notebooks of Lectures at the Jardin des Plantes, Paris (MS), 1810–1811.

Peale, Charles Willson (1741–1827)

Self-Portrait, 1777–1778. Oil on canvas, 12 3/4 x 12 1/2 in.

*Bald Eagle (Haliaeetus leucocephalus). Collected by Alexander Wilson, Great Egg Harbor, New Jersey, probably in January 1811. MCZ [Plate 3, this catalogue]

*Two Golden Pheasants (Chrysolophus pictus). Gift of George Washington to Peale's Museum, 1786. MCZ [Plate 4, this catalogue]

*Wild Turkey (Meleagris gallopavo). Probably collected by Titian Ramsay Peale on the Stephen H. Long Expedition to the Rocky Mountains, 1819–1820. MCZ [Plate 3, this catalogue]

"Directions for preserving Birds, &c.," copied July or August 1787 from a taxidermy pamphlet by L. J. M. Daubenton that Peale received from Benjamin Franklin. In Peale's *Letter Book* (MS), vol. 2, 1782.

With Titian Ramsay Peale. *The Long Room, Interior of Front Room in Peale's Museum*, 1822 (facsimile exhibited). Watercolor and ink, 14 x 20 3/4 in. DIA

Admission Ticket to Peale's Museum, ca. 1821–1822. Etching, 3 1/8 x 4 7/8 in.

Gift Solicitation Form for Peale's Museum (Draft of Letter to Mrs. Morrison, Tennessee, March 17, 1805). Engraved by James Akin; illustration hand-colored by Elizabeth Peale; manuscript additions by Rubens Peale, 9 5/8 x 7 3/4 in.

Skeleton of the Mammoth is Now to Be Seen At the Museum.... Philadelphia: John Ormrod, 1801 or 1802. Broadside, 11 3/4 x 9 1/8 in.

Peale, Rembrandt (1778–1860)

A Short Account of the Behemoth or Mammoth, 1802. Broadside, 17 5/8 x 7 in.

With John Isaac Hawkins (1772–1854), composer. *"The Beauties of Creation."* Sheet music for song accompanying C. W. Peale's *Discourse Introductory to a Course of Lectures on the Science of Nature...*. Philadelphia: Zachariah Poulson, Jr., 1800.

Peale, Titian Ramsay
(1799–1885)

Burrowing Owl and Cliff Swallow (Athene cunicularia and Hirundo pyrrhonota), n.d. Graphite and wash, 13 3/8 x 10 1/8 in. ALS

Colorado Chipmunks (Tamias quadrivittatus) ("Sc. quadrivittatus Natural size Specimen obtained at the Rocky mountains by TRP."), July 28, 1820. Watercolor and graphite, 7 1/4 x 9 5/8 in.

Dog-Day or Annual Cicadas (genus Tibicen), ca. 1819–1820. Watercolor, graphite, and ink, 7 1/4 x 5 3/8 in.

Eastern Red Bat (Lasiurus borealis), ca. 1819–1820. Watercolor and graphite, 11 x 8 1/2 in.

Four-Horned Sphinx or Elm Sphinx Caterpillars (Ceratomia amyntor) ("Ceratomia quadricornis H."), 1817. Watercolor and graphite, 10 x 8 1/8 in.

Grizzly Bears (Ursus arctos horribilis) ("Missouri Bear. Ursus horribilis: Ord."), ca. 1822. Watercolor, graphite, and ink, 7 1/4 x 9 1/2 in.

Largemouth Bass (Micropterus salmoides) ("No 1 New Orleans...Nov 1820"), 1820. Watercolor and graphite, 5 3/8 x 8 1/2 in.

Long-Horned Grasshopper (family Tettigoniidae) ("Carthagena April 4 1831 Nat. size coloured from the living Specn...."), 1831. Watercolor and graphite, 9 x 5 1/2 in.

*Mastodon Skeleton (Mammut americanum), 1821. Graphite, ink, and wash, 14 3/8 x 19 in. [Figure 16, this catalogue]

Mink and Ermine (Mustela vison and Mustela erminia), ca. 1819–1820. Watercolor and graphite, 8 7/8 x 6 3/4 in.

Monarch Butterfly (Danaus plexippus) with Chrysalids and Caterpillar, 1817. Watercolor, graphite, and ink, 9 7/8 x 8 in.

Muskrats (Ondatra zibethicus) ("Mus. Zibethicus"), 1819–1820. Watercolor and graphite, 6 7/8 x 9 1/4 in.

Wild Turkey (Meleagris gallopavo), n.d. Engraving by Alexander Lawson, 14 1/8 x 10 3/4 in. ALS

Circular of the Philadelphia Museum: Containing Directions for the Preparation and Preservation of Objects of Natural History. Philadelphia: James Kay, Jr., 1831.

Peck, William Dandridge
(1763–1822)

*Lumpsucker or Lumpfish (Cyclopterus lumpus). Collected ca. 1793. MCZ [Figure 7, this catalogue]

White Perch (Morone americana) ("Labrax Rufus") and Yellow Perch (Perca flavescens). Collected ca. 1790. MCZ

Poe, Edgar Allan (1809–1849)

The Conchologist's First Book: A System of Testaceous Malacology, Arranged Expressly for the Use of Schools.... Philadelphia: Haswell, Barrington, and Haswell, 1840.

Potts, Serena M. (1812–1898?)

"With Pencil and Brush" (Botanical Illustrations), vol. 2, 1857–1891. Watercolor, graphite, and ink. UPENN

Pursh, Frederick (1774–1820)

Copper Iris (Iris fulva), n.d. Watercolor and graphite, 18 3/8 x 11 1/2 in. BDC

Large Roundleaved Orchid (Platanthera or Habenaria orbiculata), n.d. Watercolor and graphite, 17 x 11 3/4 in. BDC

*Mountain Laurel (Kalmia latifolia), n.d. Watercolor and graphite, 13 1/4 x 8 1/8 in. BDC [Plate 14, this catalogue]

Small Bonny Bellflower or Southern Harebell (Campanula divaricata), n.d. Watercolor and graphite, 12 7/8 x 7 3/4 in. BDC

Rafinesque, C. S. (Constantine Samuel) (1783–1840)

*Creeping Eryngo (Eryngium prostratum) ("Streblanthus auriculatus...half Natural Size"), n.d. Graphite and ink, 7 3/4 x 6 1/4 in. [Figure 20, this catalogue]

*"Description of the Streblanthus, a New American Genus of Plants—and Enquiries on its Natural Affinities" (MS), n.d. [Figure 20, this catalogue]

"Graphic Systems of America: Analytical—Simple Signs—found in the Linapi Wallamolum" (MS), 1833.

Advertisement for Rafinesque's *Autikon Botanikon*, from his *Atlantic Journal and Friend of Knowledge* (Vol. 1, Nos. 3–4). Philadelphia, 1832.

A Monograph of the Fluviatile Bivalve Shells of the River Ohio.... Philadelphia: J. Dobson, 1832.

Tabular View of the Compared Atlantic Alphabets & Glyphs of Africa & America. Philadelphia, 1832. Broadside, 10 1/2 x 7 in.

Say, Thomas (1787–1834)

Hoppner Meyer, after J. Wood. *Portrait of Thomas Say*, n.d. Engraving, 9 x 5 3/8 in.

Prospectus for *American Entomology, or Descriptions of the Insects of North America....* Philadelphia: Mitchell and Ames, 1817.

Schweinitz, Lewis David von (1780–1834)

Synopsis Fungorum Carolinae Superioris: Secundum Observationes. [Leipzig?], 1822. Reprinted from *Schriften der Naturforschenden Gesellschaft zu Leipzig*, vol. 1.

Seymour, I. H.

Venus Flytrap (Dionaea muscipula), n.d. Hand-colored engraving, after John Ellis, 8 3/4 x 5 3/8 in. BDC

Smith, Charles Hamilton

The Natural History of the Human Species.... London: W. H. Allen, 1847 (?).

Stephens, Henry Louis (1824–1882)

The Comic Natural History of the Human Race. Philadelphia: S. Robinson, 1851. LCP

Swan (Native American Leader)

Pictographic Signature Collected by John Halkett in Washington, D.C. (MS), 1822. WLC

Thoreau, Henry David (1817–1862)

American Climbing Fern (Lygodium palmatum). Collected in the Ministerial Swamp, Concord, Massachusetts, in 1851 or after (first mentioned in Thoreau's *Journal* on November 24, 1851). GH

Thornton, Robert John (1768–1837)

A New Illustration of the Sexual System of Linnaeus..., vol. 1. London: T. Bensley, 1799.

Titford, William Jowit (1784–1823?)

Sketches Towards a Hortus Botanicus Americanus.... London: Sherwood, Neely, and Jones, 1811.

Torrey, John (1796–1873) and **Asa Gray** (1810–1888)

A Flora of North America: Containing Abridged Descriptions of all the Known Indigenous and Naturalized Plants Growing North of Mexico; Arranged According to the Natural System, vol. 1. New York: Wiley and Putnam, 1838–1840.

Townsend, John Kirk
(1809–1851)

Colorado Chipmunk (Tamias quadrivittatus). Collected in the Rocky Mountains on Nathaniel Jarvis Wyeth's expedition to the Pacific Northwest, 1834. ANSP

Northern Flicker (Colaptes auratus) ("Colaptes mexicanus"). Probably collected on Nathaniel Jarvis Wyeth's expedition to the Pacific Northwest, 1834. ANSP

Turpin, P. J. F. (Pierre Jean François) (1775–1840)

Canada Lily (Lilium canadense), n.d. Watercolor and graphite, 18 1/4 x 11 1/2 in. BDC

Cucumbertree Magnolia (Magnolia acuminata), after 1797. Watercolor, graphite, and ink, 15 1/4 x 9 3/4 in. BDC

Flowers (family Theaceae?), n.d. Ink, watercolor with white bodycolor, and graphite, 13 3/4 x 12 3/8 in. BDC

Skunk Cabbage (Symplocarpus foetidus) ("Dracontium fatidum"), n.d. Watercolor, graphite, and ink, 15 1/8 x 9 3/4 in. BDC

Twinleaf (Jeffersonia diphylla), n.d. Watercolor, graphite, and ink, 15 1/4 x 9 3/4 in. BDC

White Screwstem (Bartonia verna), n.d. Hand-colored engraving, 9 5/8 x 6 in. BDC

Williams, Charles (1796–1866)

The Vegetable World. Boston: James B. Dow, 1833.

Wilson, Alexander (1766–1813)

Thomas Sully. *Portrait of Alexander Wilson*, ca. 1809–1813. Formerly attributed to Rembrandt Peale. Oil on wood panel, 20 1/2 x 16 5/8 in.

Carolina Parakeet (Conuropsis carolinensis) ("Carolina Parrot"). Date of collection unknown. MCZ

Belted Kingfisher (Ceryle alcyon), n.d. Graphite, 8 1/4 x 10 3/4 in. ALS

Eastern Screech Owl, Red Phase (Otus Asio) ("Red Owl"), n.d. Watercolor and graphite, 9 x 6 1/4 in. EML

Ruffed Grouse (Bonasa umbellus), n.d. Watercolor and graphite, 13 1/8 x 16 3/8 in. EML

Bald Eagle (Haliaeetus leucocephalus) ("White-headed Eagle"), 1830 or 1871. Hand-colored engraving by Alexander Lawson (later impression), 10 7/8 x 14 5/8 in. ALS

*American Ornithology; or, The Natural History of the Birds of the United States..., 9 vols. Philadelphia: Bradford and Inskeep, 1808–1814. Exhibited: six volumes, in rotation. [Plate 15, this catalogue]

The Foresters: A Poem, Descriptive of a Pedestrian Journey to the Falls of Niagara, in the Autumn of 1804. West Chester, Pennsylvania: Joseph Painter, 1838.

Wistar, Caspar (1761–1818)

"A Description of the Bones deposited, by the President, in the Museum of the Society...," Transactions of the APS, vol. 4 (old series), 1799.

Wordsworth, William (1770–1850)

The Complete Poetical Works of William Wordsworth.... Philadelphia: James Kay, Jr..., 1839 (copyright 1837). LCP

Wright, Asher (1803–1875)

Elementary Reading Book in Seneca (Diuhsáwahgwah Gayádoshah...). [Boston: Crocker], 1836.

Index

PLATE 1 Charles Willson Peale, *The Artist in His Museum*, 1822. Courtesy of the Pennsylvania Academy of the Fine Arts, Philadelphia. Gift of Mrs. Sarah Harrison (The Joseph Harrison, Jr. Collection).

PLATE 2 Charles Willson Peale, *Charles Waterton*, 1824. National Portrait Gallery, London.

PLATE 3 Charles Willson Peale, *Wild Turkey (Meleagris gallopavo)*. Probably collected by T. R. Peale on the Stephen H. Long Expedition to the Rocky Mountains, 1819–1820. *Bald Eagle (Haliaeetus leucocephalus)*. Collected by Alexander Wilson in Great Egg Harbor, New Jersey, probably in January 1811. Museum of Comparative Zoology, Harvard University. Photograph by Mark Sloan.

PLATE 4 Charles Willson Peale, *Two Golden Pheasants (Chrysolophus pictus)*. Gift of George Washington to Peale's Museum, 1787. Museum of Comparative Zoology, Harvard University.

PLATE 5 Whipcord, *The Fly Catching Macaroni* (Joseph Banks). Hand-colored etching, M. Darly, publisher, July 12, 1772. Colonial Williamsburg.

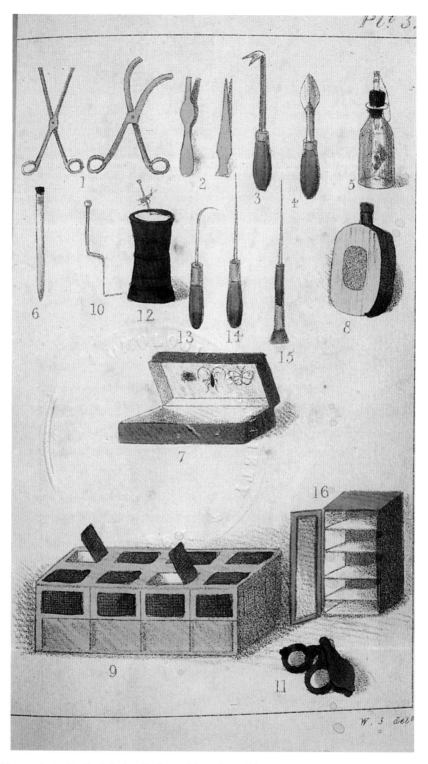

PLATE 6 Abel Ingpen, *Instructions for Collecting, Rearing, and Preserving British & Foreign Insects.* . . . London: William Smith, 1839.
Plate 3. The Academy of Natural Sciences of Philadelphia, Ewell Sale Stewart Library. Photograph by Will Brown.

PLATE 7 Titian Ramsay Peale, *Butterfly Box* (assembled). The Academy of Natural Sciences of Philadelphia.

Photograph by Will Brown.

PLATE 8 Mark Catesby, *Bead Snake (Study for Vol. 2, Plate 60 of The Natural History...)*, n.d. The Pierpont Morgan Library, New York. Gift of Henry S. Morgan, 1961.6:1.

PLATE 9 Mark Catesby, *The Natural History of Carolina, Florida, and the Bahama Islands...*, vol. 2 (2nd ed.). London: C. Marsh...,
1754. Appendix, Plate 20: *American Bison (Bos bison) ("Bison Americanus") and Bristly Locust or Rose Acacia (Robinia hispida)
("Pseudo Acacia bispida floribus roseis")*. Pennsylvania Horticultural Society, on deposit at the American Philosophical Society.

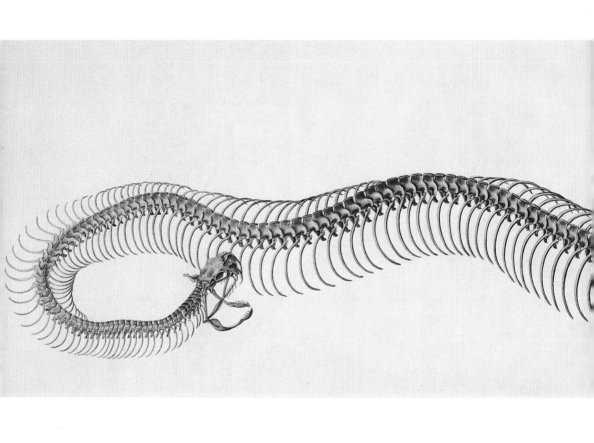

PLATE 10 Attributed to Benjamin Henry Latrobe, *Rattlesnake Skeleton*, n.d. Formerly attributed to B. S. Barton. Watercolor, graphite, and glaze. American Philosophical Society.

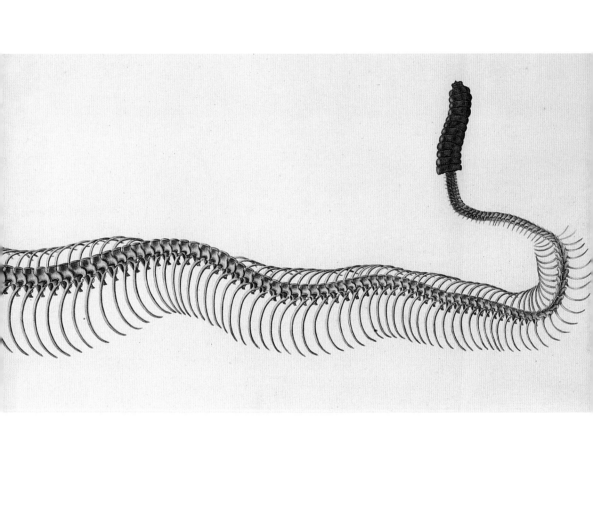

PLATE 11 William Bartram, *Rosebud Orchid, Whorled Pogonia or Purple Fiveleaf Orchid, Venus Flytrap, and Round-Leaf Sundew, with Philadelphia in Background (Cleistes divaricata, Isotria verticillata, Dionea muscipula, Drosera rotundifolia)* ("*Arethusa divaricata…*"), 1796. Brown ink. American Philosophical Society.

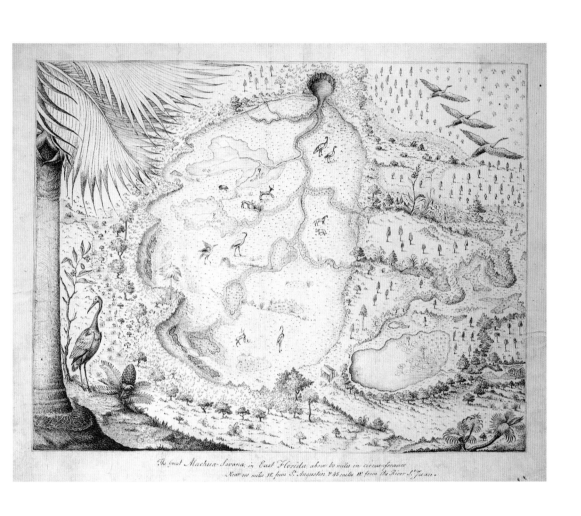

The Great Alachua-Savana, in East Florida, above 60 miles in circumference.
Near 100 miles W. from St. Augustin & 45 miles W. from the River St. Jean.

PLATE 12 William Bartram, *The Great Alachua-Savana in East Florida...*, n. d. Brown and black ink. American Philosophical Society.

PLATE 13   Mark Catesby, *The Natural History of Carolina, Florida, and the Bahama Islands...*, vol. 2 (2nd ed.).
London: C. Marsh..., 1754. Appendix, Plate 1: *Ground Hen with Meadia*. Pennsylvania Horticultural Society, on deposit
at the American Philosophical Society.

PLATE 14 Frederick Pursh, *Mountain Laurel (Kalmia latifolia)*, n.d. Watercolor and graphite. American Philosophical Society.

PLATE 15 Alexander Wilson, *American Ornithology; or, The Natural History of the Birds of the United States...*,
9 vols. Philadelphia: Bradford and Inskeep, 1808–1814. Hand-colored engraving by Alexander Lawson and others,
Vol. 1, Plate VI. American Philosophical Society.